Key to the 150 Psalms &
the 72 Genies of the Cabala

UNICURSAL

Copyright © 2024 Marc-André Ricard
maricard.com

Éditions Unicursal Publishers
unicursal.ca

ISBN 978-2-89806-600-9 (PB)
ISBN 978-2-89806-601-6 (HC)

First English Edition, Imbolc 2024

All Rights Reserved for All Countries.

No part of this publication may be reproduced or transmitted in any form or by any means, electronic or mechanical, including photocopying, recording, or by any information storage and retrieval system, without permission in writing from the editor or the author.

Key to the 150 Psalms and the 72 Genies of the Cabala

Being a faithful transcription in every respect of an 18th century text of Angelic Magic from the Ms. Français 14788.

EDITED, TRANSCRIBED & SEALS

BY

M-A RICARD

UNICURSAL

PREFACE
to this second edition.

This is the second time such that a thing has happened to me in more than thirty years of writing, but it seems that the Great Heaven has a sense of humour of his own, for shortly after completing this book, when it had just been published, I got my hands on a second source of the *Key to the 150 Psalms of David*, a manuscript copy catalogued as Ms. Français 14784.

At last, I was able to check my numerous annotations as well as any inconsistencies encountered in the main text. Even more, being of an exemplary calligraphy, this discovery came at the right time, because I could now fill in the gaps and understand some of the poorly written or simply illegible, ink-stained sentences.

Since my work at this point was limited to being a transcription of the Ms. Français 14788, I felt comfortable offering it as it stood to the general public, given that it had been transcribed with care and attention to detail. However, even with the most perfect accuracy, reproducing errors helps to perpetuate those same errors. That is why, when the time came to work on this English translation of this manuscript, on this Key to the Psalms, I immediately seized the opportunity to correct the shortcomings of my previous work by including the insights provided by this second manuscript source.

By comparing the two manuscripts side by side, I was able to notice certain inconsistencies in the Names and Characters of the Intelligences. Sometimes it was just a slight difference in spelling, sometimes the names were just not the same.

To this end, I have added at the end of this edition a practical comparative table of the Names of Intelligences in order to help the reader compare the variations between the two manuscripts.

As for the Magical Characters, these were sometimes very different from one source to another, giving the impression that they were copied from a text where the ink had been partially erased. Another point, I also noticed a discrepancy in the numbering of the Psalms; that is to say, in some places a Psalm could be offset by more or less two places in comparison with the second manuscript. For example, in one, it is numbered 70th, whereas in the second it corresponds to 69th, and so on. The problem here is that, in the absence of a third source to determine which of the two texts is in error, we can only move forward and leave everything as it is to the good care of the reader, who will, if he pleases, have the task of pursuing my comparative research.

Until then, putting all these considerations aside, I am pleased to offer you this second annotated, corrected and expanded edition. May my efforts to improve this little book serve you well.

✠

One last thing, the French version uses the possessive pronoun *"son"* throughout the text for the Psalms as well as the Intelligences and Characters. Although I consider an Intelligence in the same way as a Spirit or an Angel, and thus a *"he"*, the use of the pronoun *"it"* was favoured as a *one pronoun fits all* only to make this translation more fluid.

INTRODUCTION.

This book is not a collection of prayers. It is a grimoire made to summon beneficial Spirits by means of their Names, their magical Characters and the Psalms.

Divided into two parts, the first entitled: *La Clef des Clavicules de Salomon des 150 Psaumes de David* (*The Key to the Clavicles of Solomon of the 150 Psalms of David*) is a small treatise from the 18th century. Written in French in 1787, it is part of three texts found in the *Ms. Français 14788*.

Today there is a plethora of works dealing with psalms and prayers in order to be noticed by the Great Heaven about our dismay and anxieties, our pressing needs and deficiencies in all areas of daily life. Despite all these methods, from the simplest to the most eccentric, one thing remains. A *sine qua non* condition, an essential ingredient must be possessed by those who wish to obtain results: *faith*.

To use this book, this Key to the Psalms, the faith essential to success —your faith— does not have to be Christian or Jewish or biblical. There is no need to confess yourself or attend Sunday mass or celebrate Shabbat. You don't need any special magical tools either, a white candle at most, if you feel so inclined, and you will be ready to undertake this mysterious Art.

You must only have faith, that is to say, possess an unshakable confidence that your operations will succeed and that through the help of the Magical Intelligences and Characters contained in this book, you will succeed in calling and conjuring these Angels, and clothe yourself with the protective mantle of a Spirit, of an invisible, powerful, and unsuspected force.

The instructions are quite simple. You will need to trace the Seals of the Intelligences which preside over miraculous operations for the particular realm where you feel the need for Heavenly assistance, then to recite the psalms corresponding to the specific days, with faith that your prayers will be heard... and answered. In a nutshell, that's the whole process.

The field of action of these Spirits is very broad and covers numerous magical operations. With their help, it will be possible to obtain protection against enemies and highway thieves, to obtain the favor of judges and high-ranking people, to deliver those who have been unjustly condemned or imprisoned, to be loved by someone, deliver a besieged city or put an end to any war, to protect oneself from dangers on land and sea, against storms and earthquakes, to cure various illnesses, to obtain answers in dreams... and much more.

True, this manuscript being over two hundred years old, it reflects the customs of an era very different from ours; especially when it is mentioned how to obtain the favor of a King or Prince. For the modern user, a Prince can also be a head of state, a company president, a manager or any person in power. Same thing about the remission of sins. We can interpret this as a request for spiritual help during depressions, when everything is wrong and going downhill, in order to see the light at the end of the tunnel, etc. It will be easy for the reader to discover more contemporary applications.

A final word about this text. You will notice that the psalms have not been reproduced in this book. I know, it's like writing a cookbook without any recipes. Since they were absent from the Manuscript, and since you probably have an old Bible stashed away somewhere at home, you will have absolutely no difficulty obtaining a copy of the psalms. This is why I carried on with the essential of the method to conduct these operations, as it was once written in the Manuscript, more than two centuries ago.

The second part of the book: *Les 72 Noms de Dieu avec des versets des Psaumes qui y répondent* (*The 72 Names of God with corresponding verses from the Psalms*), provides a guide for working with the same psalms, but in using a different approach. This short text catalogs the seventy-two names of God or Cabalistic Angels, with the verses specific to each of them. Although there is no specific ways explained in the text, the least ingenious reader will quickly find a way to take advantage of the information contained therein.

I briefly address the topic of the *Schemhamphorash* (or *Schema Hamphorash*, as Eliphas Lévi said) in my recent work on the Clavicles of King Solomon. As I explained then, the application and implementation of the Tetragrammaton יהוה through the Schemhamphorash, or the "Name of God explained," are represented by seventy-two names, which individually correspond to what occultists and cabalists describe as *Cabalistic Genies*. As for those uninitiated, they give them the name of *Guardian Angels*.

The general idea is that God, being the first cause of all things, his name, composed of four letters: *Yod, He, Vau, He*, contains everything that exists; the immensity of God contained in his ineffable name. The wise cabalists were able to calculate by gematria, according to the value of letters and numbers, that the sum of seventy-two corresponded, among other things, to as many divine attributes; each being expressed and bodily, so to speak, manifested by a Genii. Several individualities which form one single consciousness. God.

In other words, addressing an Angel or a Cabalistic Genii is nothing other than addressing God directly, but through one of his multiple facets personified by a Celestial Intelligence.

Vast science that is Cabala, I would not like to deviate from my initial goal and bore the reader with a complex presentation which, at times, could feel like a course in esoteric mathematics. Consequently, in order not to overly burden this introduction, I will simply mention that by certain processes, it was possible to determine which parts of the psalms correspond to the Angels or Genies. And from there, it is easy to consult who is the ruler for that specific psalm.

Please note that even in this simplified form, it is not essential to be aware of what I have just mentioned to achieve convincing results. However, the reader wishing to walk a few steps, even uncertain, on the path of Cabala will certainly be able to admire the full extent of this science by consulting various works, including two that I would suggest: *The Cabala* by Papus, or even *The Cabalistic Science* by Lenain.

▸ *Of the Ms. Français 14788* ◂

The Manuscript used for this transcription of this book is called *Mélanges astrologiques* (*Astrological Mixtures*). It is kept at the Bibliothèque de l'Arsenal (*Arsenal Library* — BnF) in Paris. The Manuscripts Department catalogs it as follows (translated):

Fol. 1. "Works of Picatrix, French translation, from Latin into French and from Spanish into Latin, based on the Arabic original in 1256. (1756.)" — Copy of ms. of the Marquis de Paulmy, today at the Arsenal Library.

Fol. 73. "Key of the clavicles of Solomon, of the 150 Psalms of David, with the characters of all the genies or spirits presiding over miraculous operations. (1787.) — F. B."

Fol. 155. "The 72 names of God, with the corresponding verses from the Psalms."

XVIIIth century. Paper. 162 sheets, 190 x 140 mm. Marbled calfskin binding.

This designation will probably mean little to most of us. On the other hand, the main work of this Manuscript, *Works of Picatrix*, is a very familiar name among occultists. Since it was customary at the time to transcribe and group several texts within a single notebook, we will understand that the works of Picatrix have no link, directly or remotely, with the Psalms of David and that is why I have put this text aside, focusing only on folios 73 to 163 to complete this transcription.

▸ *Of the Ms. Français 14784* ◂

Initially, this manuscript was not part of my original work. It was only following a strange combination of circumstances that I discovered this text, just as I had completed this very book.

Having subsequently used it extensively for purposes of comparison and correction, this manuscript has been extremely helpful in filling in many gaps.

Also kept at the Arsenal Library, it is archived as follows:

14784. "La vraye Cabale mistérieuse et divine pour l'intelligence des 150 psaumes de... David... "

XVIIIth century.. Paper. 87 sheets, 218 by 160 millimeters. Hardback. (French Supplement 1113.)

According to the notes found throughout the text, this manuscript is the result of an older copy. Unfortunately the trail ends just as quickly since nothing points to its origin. This manuscript also includes numerous variations in the Characters of the Intelligences. I would have liked to have a third copy on hand in order to verify each of them more precisely, however, we will have to limit ourselves to those of Ms. 14788.

▸ *How to summon Genies* ◂

Since this Manuscript does not include any specific ritual or procedure to summon the Spirits and Genies of the psalms, I thought it would be helpful to provide you one that is easy to follow; this is the one I personally use when I want to practice in the greatest simplicity.

Setting aside all considerations about planetary hours, the course of the stars in the sky or the lunar phases, unless this is specified in the

Manuscript; when you have found the appropriate Genii for the situation in which you are about to practice this call, find a calm and serene place, far from any disturbances.

Light a nice quality incense as well as a white candle, then gaze at the flame for a short time.

Take a few deep breaths and clear your mind. Center yourself. There is only the flame that burns and you.

Then think of the name of the Genii to evoke. Repeat his name mentally as you write his Name and trace his Character on a piece of white paper, parchment, or as prescribed in the Manuscript.

Then gaze at the Character. Take a deep breath, place your right hand on your heart and chant the psalm, the number of times as indicated in the text.

When you're done, take one last breath. Thank the Genii, make the *Triple Sign*, if you know how, or a simple greeting gesture, then extinguish the candle by pinching the flame between your fingers.

Dispose of the Character as directed or store it in an appropriate location, along with your materials, until the next occasion.

✠

I hope this little ritual will be useful to you or that it will inspire you to create your own. If you already have developed your own method, then so much the better. I encourage you to use it.

May this book be precious to you so that your calls to the Angels be positively answered. May the Genies come to your aid and to your loved ones, in the light and glory of the One.

M-A Ricard ~555

Ostara[+9], 2023.

CLEF

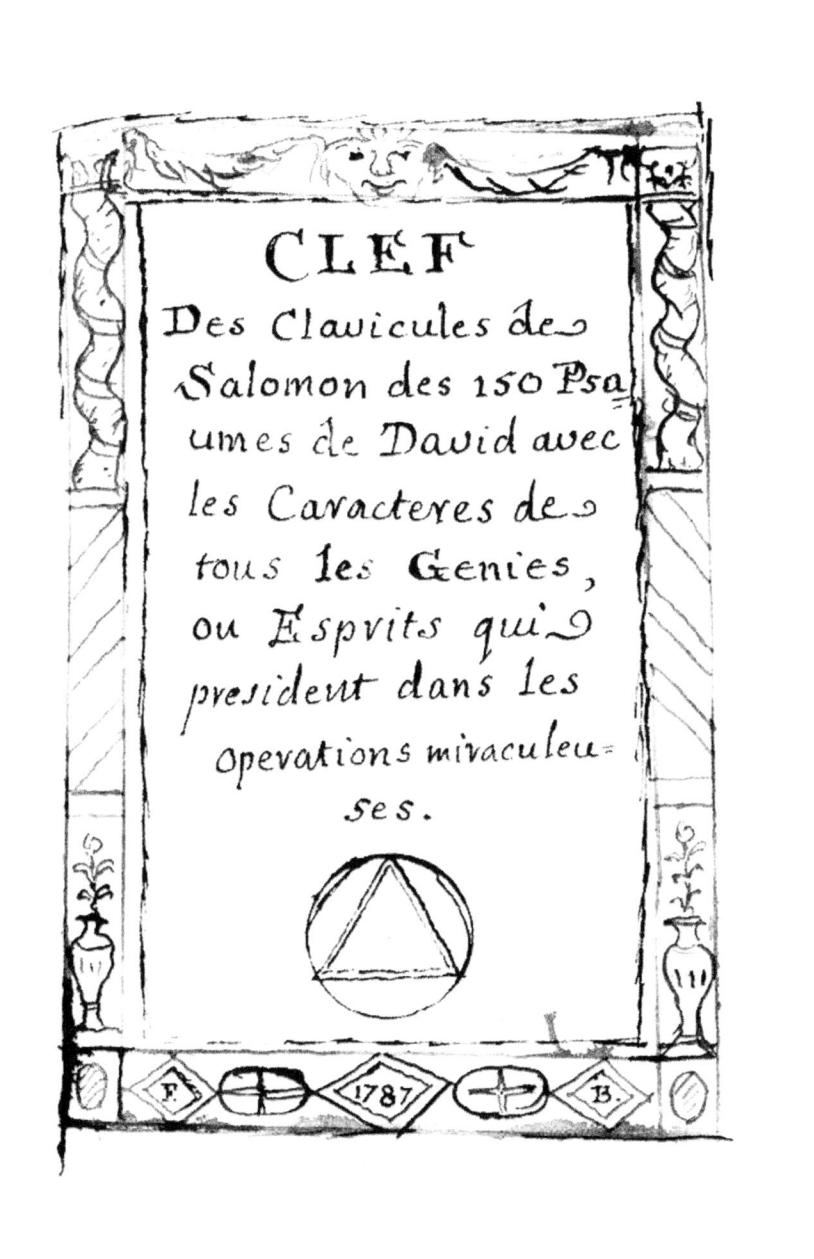

Des Clavicules de Salomon des 150 Psaumes de David avec les Caracteres de tous les Genies, ou Esprits qui president dans les operations miraculeuses.

Elohim
Agla
Adonay
Jehovah
Schemhammaphoras

FIRST PSALM.

Through the Psalms, one can acquire true Theology, the art of preaching and giving good advice and prayers for the conversion of the Leviticus according to St Isidore who will say it 22 days in a row, and then after a good confession, good works, fasts and alms, will see an Angel of God who will teach him how he should govern his affairs for the glory of God, and his Salvation. It also serves to avoid bad company and find good ones. It is good for health, to be guaranteed from the hand of one's enemies. It should be written on [Kid[1]] parchment up to the verse: *et omnia quæcumque*[2], on a Thursday at the hour of Jupiter, then your name, and below that of the Intelligence and its Character, and write

---

1 *Chevreau*. Young goat. Same throughout the text.
2 End of verse 3.

the rest of the Psalm on turquoise-blue cotton paper, and below the name of your enemy or contraries, then writing: *I who am such son of such* ✠ *be far from me all untoward things.* Then sew the two writings together from the paper and parchment into a piece of taffeta and hang it from the collar.

Name of Intelligence: **ELPAD**

Its Character:

PSALM 2.

It is [used] against the evil intentions of all the wicked. St Isidore assures us that whoever says it devoutly will be well received by the Great. If we say it over a sick person he will heal, and if we find ourselves in peril at sea. Write it on the remains[3] of an earthenware pot, and say it three times, then throw it into the sea; it will calm down.

Name of Intelligence: **GHOLAM**

Its Character:

---

3   *Sur un rest*, in the Ms. Probably a piece or shard.

PSALM 3.

It guarantees against the malice of domestic enemies. St Isidore assured us that he who says it will be at peace with all his enemies. It is also used to heal the sick, saying it over him with faith and devotion. It is good against all kinds of perils, against bad dreams, evil thoughts and temptations, to turn away from committing sins or crimes against Prince and other powers. One must rise with the Sun, and say this Psalm 7 times, and at the end of each time say the name of the Intelligence; and for more strength and virtue, write it with the name of the Intelligence and its Character with ink prepared with a little Rose water[4].

Name of Intelligence: **MAGAN**

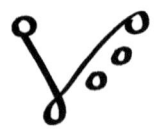

Its Character:

---

4 *Eau Rose*, thus written throughout the Ms. It is understood that it is actually *Rose Water*.

PSALM 4.

It is used against tribulations, to acquire the friendship of the Great. That is why one must rise on a Thursday with the Sun, and say it 7 times with the name of the Intelligence, write the name and Character in the left hand, and before speaking to people, say and look fixedly at what is in hand, then afterwards speak with assurance.

Name of Intelligence: **HA**

Its Character:

PSALM 5.

It is used to gain the friendship of great Lords. Take some olive oil on which you will say the Psalm three times, and each time the name of the Intelligence. Then rub this oil on your forehead, and on the underside of your hand, on which you will have written the name of the Intelligence and the Character, and you will see the effect.

Name of Intelligence: **CAMIEL**

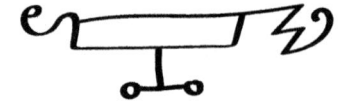

Its Character:

PSALM 6.

Comforts the torments of the mind [and] eye sickness. St Isidore says that saying it 3 times in succession with confidence and devotion, it changes a Judge's ill will and prevents him from condemning unjustly. It is good against the labours and torments of the mind, saying it 7 times when in need, naming each time the Intelligence, and then saying: *I pray unto thee Jesus, Lord of Salvation, by the virtue of these st names and these Psalms to deliver me from such torment or evil, from which thou can cure and deliver those who please thee.*

It is good against eye sickness, if said 7 times, three days in a row with its Intelligence, and each time written on a lettuce leaf from which to rub the eyes.

Name of Intelligence: **ISII**

Its Character:

PSALM 7.

It serves against enemies and lawsuits, carrying it with its Character. And if pursued by someone, take some earth and say the following Psalm, and throw it in front with the Name of the Intelligence, and he will turn away. But if you have a specific enemy, take a piece of new crockery full of fountain or river water, and say over it 4 times from the verse: *Exurge Domine in irâ tuâ*, to the end and add to it: *My God this is how thou put down thy enemy Dahahabaile and trampled underfoot the hatred between me and so-and-so*. And then throw this water where your enemy often walks and you'll see him running after you[5]. If you have a lawsuit, it must be said before your Judges, and name the Intelligence; you will gain their favour.

Name of Intelligence: **EHEB**

Its Character:

---

5 Obviously, the author meant the enemy will flee the operator at full speed rather than start pursuing him!

PSALM 8.

David depicts in this Psalm Jesus Christ and his divinity. This is the way to give thanks to God. It lifts our spirit toward God, and makes us follow his will. It is used to give rest to the mind and body, and to soothe a crying child, saying it over him 3 times with its Intelligence, and putting its Character on him; he will be soothed and guaranteed of all evils. You can do the same on yourself if you want to rest.

Name of Intelligence: **EJAT**

Its Character:

PSALM 9.

David asks God in this Psalm to forgive him on Judgment Day. If you say it devoutly, it brings hidden things to light and confirms faith. The ancients St Jerome and St Augustine say that it will bring about [the] favour of a great Lord; it is also used to heal a sick child.

Name of Intelligence: **HYASA**

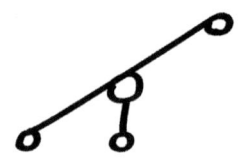

Its Character:

PSALM 10.

David did it when persecuted by his enemies, who forced him to kill King Moab. And by the virtue of this Psalm, God made him hear through the Prophet Gad of his return to his Kingdom, and of his victory. If this Psalm is said devoutly before an altar in a Church, or other places, St Hieronymus assures us that it delivers a person possessed by the devil, saying it 3 times over him. It makes one flee from his enemies, and assassins, saying it 3 times with its Intelligence, looking to Heaven, tracing with one hand on the other its Character, or putting the first two fingers one on the other, or bending them a little.

Name of Intelligence: **ZILOZ**

Its Character:

PSALM 11.

David made this Psalm fleeing from Saul, who had besieged him in Mount Zeph, by whose virtue he was delivered by the grace of God, as said in the First of Kings, Chap. 3. It gives divine help. St Cassiodorus assures the healing of a sick person, being said three times over him, and his soul will be delivered from mortal sins. It prevents one from being deceived by flatterers and bad advice. It is used to resolve doubtful matters. It has to be said 3 times with the name of the Intelligence and written with the Character. One must look fixedly while saying it, and the first thought one will get at the end of the 3rd time is the best one to follow.

Name of Intelligence: **GABAJH**

Its Character:

PSALM 12.

David did so fearing the destruction of Jerusalem, which had already happened, and for the establishment of which the Jews said it with great devotion. When said devoutly before a crucifix, it has the virtue of restoring to their country those who have been driven out. Those who say it every day will be delivered from sudden and violent death. It is to be written with the Intelligence on a Sunday at the first hour of the day, and the Character, with a prepared pen and ink, then folded, and on the first fold, write the Intelligence; and fold and refold with a linen thread, then carry it wrapped in cloth.

Name of Intelligence: **NEKAH**

Its Character:

PSALM 13.

David composed this Psalm against King Nebuchadnezzar. It is good against the ungrateful, superb and blasphemous. It serves to deliver prisoners and those who find themselves in some bad encounters, and to restrain the wicked tongues of backbiters and false witnesses. And if anyone doubts of being falsely accused, he must say it 3 times a day with the name of the Intelligence and its Character, which you must look at fixedly while saying it, then speak whoever will against you, no faith will be added to the bad speech.

Name of Intelligence: **EATOR**

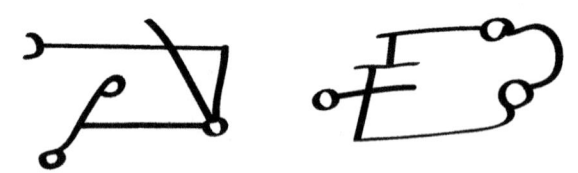

Its Character:

PSALM 14.

David made it when he resolved to build the Temple. Whoever wants to raise some buildings must say it 3 times with its Intelligence and its Character, and write it on wood or stone, and put it in the foundations; it will last forever. He who says it often will be maintained in his condition and prosperity. It is also good against evil Spirits. Whoever says it over an earthen vessel full of water, naming the Intelligence and writing the name on the vessel with a knife; and if one fears the Spirit or someone, one must wash one's face and hands with the said water; they will not be able to harm it.

Name of Intelligence: **ELY**

Its Character[6]:

---

6   Same Character as Ps. 67. Same for Ms. 14784.

PSALM 15.

David made it prophesying the coming of Jesus Christ. Whoever says it devoutly, will obtain health of the body. He who says it every day cannot be deceived in his affairs. It is used to reconcile with enemies and to find out who has stolen something. Take earth from the river and sand, and make a ball of dough and wrap in it the names of those you suspect each in a separate, well-folded piece of paper, and write at the bottom of the earthen vessel the name of the Intelligence and the Character. Then fill it and put the ball in it, then say the Psalm over it with its Intelligence saying: *My God, let me know who has stolen such and such a thing from me.* And the paper that will surface will be the one who stole from you.

Name of Intelligence: **CAA**

Its Character:

PSALM 16.

David composed this Psalm when Saul was pursuing him, as did many others in similar circumstances. It is good for the torments of the body and mind, and has the same virtues as the previous one. It is used by travellers to travel happily. If worn written with its Intelligence and Character under the left armpit, and pronounce it nine times, you won't have any bad encounters, and you will be pleasant to everyone.

Name of Intelligence: **SCEMA**

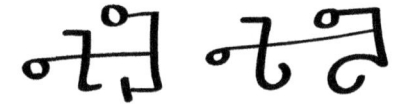

Its Character:

PSALM 17.

David gives thanks to God in this Psalm for his victory over his enemies (1st of Kings, Chap. 3). It is good against lightning and thunder, from which one will not be offended, saying it kneeling when it thunders. It is good against highway robbers, if you say it with its Intelligence and while walking. You can engrave its Character wherever you like with a knife and the name of the Intelligence, and they will not harm you.

Name of Intelligence: **JELA**

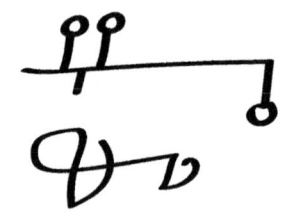

Its Character:

PSALM 18.

David in this one expresses the greatness of God and his Law. It is good for acquiring God's grace. If a Preacher says it 3 times with its Intelligence and Character, he will not fail in his sermon. It makes it easier for women to give birth by taking a bit of soil from the path, then writing it down until the verse: *Tu es quem spiritus*, with its Intelligence and Character, and putting it on the woman's body, then saying it 3 times; she will give birth in the moment. And as soon as she gives birth, remove it immediately.

Name of Intelligence: **MECHEL**

Its Character:

It is good for raising one's spirit. For this, take a glass of wine and honey, and say the Psalm over it 7 times, each time saying: *Mechel, I conjure thee, give me a good spirit and understanding*. In all other studies and science, say it on a Wednesday or Friday at sunrise, and give it to drink to whomever you wish.

PSALM 19.

David made this Psalm in time of war (2. Kings, Chap. 21) to ask God for victory over his enemies. That is why it is used during wartime, and whoever says it will get what he wants from God. If it is said over a sick person, the reason for the illness will be known. If he rests that day, he will live. If he is worried, he will die. If you fight your enemy, you must write it on Goat parchment with the blood of a black Rooster, signed on the day and hour of Mars, then bind it with a wire, and wear it around your neck. When you'll want to fight, say the Psalm in the morning.

Name of Intelligence: **JEHEU**

Its Character:

PSALM 20.

St Cassiodorus claims that this Psalm calmed popular dissension; if it is said devoutly for 3 days. And it even serves to have a long life and to be well received by everyone.

Name of Intelligence: **MELEE**

Its Character:

PSALM 21.

It is good to obtain God's grace. It is used to free prisoners by saying it for 3 days. It calms those who are angry with us. It is used against the perils of the sea. And if we say it at the entrance of a house where there are Spirits and wrongdoers, and if we want to get out of prison, we must say it three times every day with its Intelligence, and having said, we must every three days, near the prison door, mark its Intelligence and Character with some instrument.

Name of Intelligence: **AZLA**

Its Character:

PSALM 22.

It protects against tyrants. It is good to have answer in dreams, like the previous one. It should be written up to the verse where it reads: *Oculi mei semper ad Dominum*, with the Intelligence and Character and request, and put it under the bedside, the sheet against the head; and observe the dream well and you will see your answer.

Name of Intelligence: **ASSA**

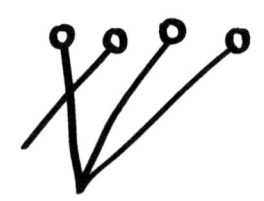

Its Character:

PSALM 23.

It is used to deliver man from afflictions; to obtain peace and God's grace, and health; and also against enemies and wild beasts. For this purpose, it should be written on Goat parchment with the Intelligence and Character, and carried and said as needed.

Name of Intelligence: **COST**

Its Character:

PSALM 24.

Those who say it will obtain from God the necessities of life. And he who treads dangerous paths will never have accidents. And if one wishes to obtain in dream an answer on something one is in trouble about, one must on Sunday and Wednesday write it on a Laurel or Ivy leaf, with ink prepared with Rose water, and the name and Character of the Intelligence. And in the evening, say it 7 times and each time, make the request; and while asleep you will have the answer in dreams.

Name of Intelligence: **GAMEOL**

Its Character:

PSALM 25.

It is good to preserve oneself in large communities where there are wicked people. It is good for consoling the afflicted and against the tricks of the devil, to free oneself from prison. Evening and morning, three times for 7 days with the Intelligence, which must be written with its Character on the door of the jailer with a knife, and be it even for the galleys, for an unknown life that one cannot imagine, he will be released.

Name of Intelligence: **JOSLEM**

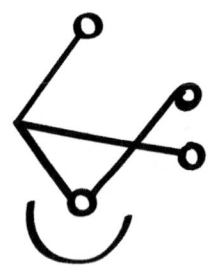

Its Character:

PSALM 26.

It is good for those called to great office. If aid devoutly every day, one will be very restful and enlightened in his conduct. It is infallible and serves all who are in charge of anything and government. It will make you choose which of the two paths you should take. If one is in a halt, one will be enlightened as soon as it is said. And it is good for making oneself master of ferocious beasts, if one writes it with its Intelligence and Character on parchment cut into a triangle △ and shows it to some wild beast, saying only the Psalm; it will tame itself like a lamb.

Name of Intelligence: **OMYA**

Its Character:

PSALM 27.

It is good for those who confess suffering for their sins, and by this means can obtain from God all they need, saying it devoutly every day. It is good for those who are persecuted by their children and relatives, for those who give alms so that their goods may be multiplied in this world and the next. It reconciles enemies. For this, you must say it 3 times with the name of the Intelligence and staring your enemy in the face, and bend the big finger on the first joint of the index, and form the Character[7] 3 times, and you will be at peace with him.

Name of Intelligence: **JELEM**

Its Character:

---

[7] *Et y former le cha... cy manque)* in the text. Ms. 14784 confirms the exact phrase.

PSALM 28.

It is good for praising God in all his works, and thanking him for all the spiritual and temporal goods received from him so that he may multiply them. It is used to guard against storms, tempests on sea and land, and their tremors, and even ferocious beasts. So take 7 Willow or Palm leaves, if you have any, on which you will say the Psalm 7 times with the name of the Intelligence, and write it with the Character on paper and fold it, after putting the leaves inside, and cover it with some cloth and carry it on your breast during your travels, and fear nothing on sea and land, nor in the deserts.

Name of Intelligence: **OLEL**

Its Character:

PSALM 29.

It is good against adultery, and to heal the sick who must not die of this disease, and even to have neither misery nor poverty in this life. Against malignant fever, write it in the patient's name on Wednesday or Sunday, at daybreak, with the Intelligence and Character, and write below: *I conjure thee _____[8] that such a son of such a daughter may soon be cured of all fevers and infirmities.* You have to say it 3 times every morning over the sick until they are cured.

Name of Intelligence: **DALFA**

Its Character:

---

[8] Empty space here in the Ms. as a placeholder for the Intelligence's name.

PSALM 30.

It is good against Demoniacs and Diabolic powers. It prevents from the evil spells that enchanters and sorcerers usually cast on children's eyes. To prevent and destroy the spell, we must say it with the name of the Intelligence on olive oil, and rub it on the forehead and the region of the heart, and form the Character on one and the other; it will prevent the eye of the sick person from having a curse, which happens quite often.

Name of Intelligence: **COSCEL**

Its Character:

PSALM 31.

It is useful to know if God has forgiven us our sins, and even against the bites of Dogs and Snakes, particularly by saying the verse: *In camo et freno maxillas eorum constringe qui non approximant ad te.*

It is also good for those who have committed hidden crimes and fear being discovered. If you say it 3 times every day with the name of the Intelligence written on your chest with the Character, one will never speak.

Name of Intelligence: **HELEM**

Its Character:

PSALM 32.

It acquires God's grace, and imparts the Law to the listeners one preaches to. It drives away temptations; prevents barrenness in women. It is suitable to relieve a besieged place by taking an earthen vessel full of olive oil, and saying the Psalm 3 times a day, on it in the morning, at noon and in the evening, with its Intelligence; and with this oil trace the name of the Intelligence and the Character against all the gates of the city, square or house, and do the same thing 7 times, and after the 7 times, one will be delivered and the siege will be lifted at the end of 7 days.

Name of Intelligence: **JOLA**

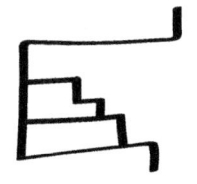

Its Character:

PSALM 33.

It delivered from the grasp of powers; students who say it devoutly every day will soon be learned. He who wishes to win his case or who desires a settlement, he must say it three mornings three times in a row, with the name of the Intelligence to be written with the Character on the back of the left arm, and such effect will be seen.

Name of Intelligence: **RINA**

Its Character:

PSALM 34.

It is good against barrenness and poverty, against the disturbance of powers and tyrants, to confound him and cause death if said devoutly every day. It brings victory in a fair fight and confusion among enemies; stops the overflow of vicious children. It should be written on parchment with the Intelligence and Character, then folding it and saying: *I pray unto thee, God of virtue, that thou make so-and-so turn back from his errors, that he leaves all vices, and only do thou will.* And then sew it into his clothes and unbeknownst to him.

Name of Intelligence: **EMER**

Its Character:

PSALM 35.

It has the virtue of the previous one; it gives consolation; it makes women give birth without any pain; it makes our goods to prosper, saying it every Thursday and Tuesday morning with its Intelligence and Character marked on an Olive tree leaf with prepared ink, and hanging it on the door of the house.

Name of Intelligence: **ALAEL**

Its Character:

PSALM 36.

It gives patience in our adversities. It confounds our enemies, so that they cannot harm us no matter how much they hate us. If we say it devoutly every Tuesday morning, and carry it written on parchment with the name and Character and name of the Intelligence.

Name of Intelligence: **RAMA**

Its Character:

PSALM 37.

Whosoever says it devoutly will obtain the remission of his sins, and exemption from the punishment he deserved. It heals from epilepsy[9] if you write it on a Silver blade with an awl, on a Wednesday morning, with its Intelligence and its Character, and make him say it 7 times a day, in the morning, at noon and in the evening, and see that he wears the blade hanging from his collar, he will heal.

Name of Intelligence: **COLY**

Its Character:

$$+ \cdot\!\!\!\!\downarrow\!\!\!\!\cdot +$$

---

9   *Mal caduc.*

PSALM 38.

It serves to acquire patience against backbiting, if said devoutly 7 times. God allows us to guess the day of our death by a few signs. If you want to argue about some science, you must say it in front with its Intelligence, and at the beginning of the argument, you must bend the index finger of the left hand in a circle for the Character, and you will find all the necessary reasons to confound your opponents.

Name of Intelligence: **VIQUA**

Its Character:

PSALM 39.

David made this Psalm to ask God for the fulfillment of his desires; that is why he who says it devoutly may obtain the same. It is good for preaching, speaking or pleading in public, saying it an hour before with its Intelligence and Character which one will write with the name on the back of the right hand, and one will speak to the liking of all.

Name of Intelligence: **PINDAR**

Its Character:

PSALM 40.

It is good for raising men to dignities and for them to be cherished by God, as was Solomon. If we write it with its Intelligence and Character on the walls of the house, all who inhabit it will obtain blessing and mercy. It is good for making peace with our enemies; for getting back what they owe us. It is good for fever, if we write it on cotton paper with its Intelligence and Character, making the first letter of each verse of another colour, and say as we fold it: *May it please thee Jehovah to cure so-and-so, son of so-and-so, from the fever.* And tie it around the collar.

Name of Intelligence: **ANENA**

Its Character:

PSALM 41.

It serves to obtain from God the effect of one's fair desires. It delivers souls from Purgatory. One can even acquire the bliss of this world here, and of the other, with all prosperity, temporal and spiritual sweetness. It makes it possible to have a true answer in a dream to whatever one desire. On Wednesday, when you want to go to bed, say it 7 times with the name of the Intelligence and say: *I pray to thee, my God, by thou holy names and by Zaca that in this night be shown to me in a dream the answer to my request which is such and such.* And lie down in white sheets, put the Character on the bedside, and you will have the answer.

Name of Intelligence: **ZACA**

Its Character:

PSALM 42.

It serves to be happy in this world and to deliver oneself from the wicked. Those who say it will never die without God's grace. It prevents evil spells and enchantments. By its virtue, it restores those who have been dismissed from office, saying it three times a day, in the morning, at midday and in the evening, for 7 days, with the name of the Intelligence and with the Character that you will gaze at while saying the Psalm, and [you] will be restored.

Name of Intelligence: **JEJORDUOSEJOR**[10]

Its Character:

---

10 I couldn't ignore such a name! By comparing with Ms. 14784 which rather indicates SCIOR, we understand that the name seems composed of two parts, namely: Jejorduo-Sejor. It should be noted that it was common to interchange I's with J's, for example: Iod & Jod, Ieovah & Jeovah, etc.

PSALM 43.

Receive consolation in our affections by saying it devoutly with arms crossed over the chest. It serves to repress our enemies, saying it on Saturday and Monday morning and evening, in default[11] of the Moon on earth with the Intelligence. And while saying this Psalm, stand on the right foot and do so for 5 days.

Name of Intelligence: **ZARIA**

Its Character:

---

[11] More likely on a *waning Moon*, a lunar phase commonly used to banish hostile influences.

PSALM 44.

If you say it every morning, you will obtain from God the graces you ask of him. It is good for the wife so that she may be loved by her husband. He who says it devoutly will be delivered from violent and shameful death, saying it on his knees before a crucifix. It is good for love, saying it on a Friday morning at sunrise, at the crescent of the Moon with the Intelligence, and writing it, the Character in the middle of the left hand and saying: *I pray thee that such and such will sincerely be interested in me, and do all my bidding.* On that day, try to touch this person with your left hand, or at least let him or her see it.

Name of Intelligence: **JEFACA**[12]

Its Character:

---

[12] JEFAVA. in the Ms. I opted for the Ms. 14784 which is better written.

PSALM 45.

It is good to comfort the afflicted; to vanquish one's enemies, war being fair. It is good to overcome Devil's temptations, and compel the husband to love his wife. If she has some of his hair and saying the Psalm over olive oil, and say it 3 times with its Intelligence. Then put the hair in the oil. Then try to rub his chest and the pulse of his arm and let her mark the Character on his forehead, then put the hair around the latch of the house, and he will love her.

Name of Intelligence: **ARŸ**

Its Character:

PSALM 46.

It makes men pleasant in their commissions by winning the friendship of those who hear them happy in trade, both for selling and buying. It is good against earthquakes, to deliver prisoners, to be loved, if one says it with its Intelligence 3 days in a row, 3 times a day at the waxing of the Moon and carrying it with him with the Character; one will be loved by all those he meets.

    Name of Intelligence: **CAFEAEN**
                             or **CAFAHEM**

Its Character:

PSALM 47.

It is good for finding theft, if you say it 30 days in a row, or more if you like. It is good for the preservation of a town, castle, house or other place, and prevents their ruin and destruction, if you write it on a stone and say it devoutly in praise of God. He who says it devoutly every day and carries it with him will be happy in all his affairs. It serves to deliver a besieged city, if you say it with the Intelligence 3 times in the morning, three days in a row over a glass of ╬[13], on which you will trace the Character with the right hand while saying the Psalm, then throw the ╬ against the walls of the city to the right of the four parts of the world.

Name of Intelligence: **MALOR**
or **MAZON**

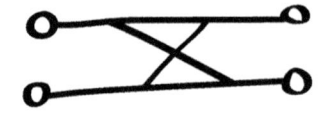

Its Character:

---

13 Thus in the text. Ms. 14784 confirms it stands for *vinegar*.

PSALM 48.

It serves for the glory of being enlightened by faith. It is used to obtain the same thing as the holy martyrs. It is good against fevers, if written on new white linen, and hung on the collar with the name of the Intelligence and Character, and said devoutly by the sick.

Name of Intelligence: **SAR**

Its Character:

PSALM 49.

It is used to make our sacrifices and alms pleasing to God, and make him answer the prayers of those who say it. It prevents us from committing mortal sins. It preserves us from the perils of the sea in storm and tempest. It guards against thieves and murderers, if one says it devoutly, and if one carries it with him with its Intelligence and Character.

Name of Intelligence: **CAIL**

Its Character:

PSALM 50.

It brings remission of sins, if said since they were committed. It is used against nosebleeds, if said devoutly for this purpose, the blood will stop. St Ambrose says this Psalm is useful for the health of the body and soul, saying it every day. And against temptations, if you say it 3 times a day with its Intelligence on linseed oil, and with this oil trace the Character over the region of the heart.

Name of Intelligence: **JESNU**

Its Character:

PSALM 51.

St Jerome says it is good against burns and against those who corrupt the Great and the Judges to the prejudice of the poor, who will be charged or punished by its virtue. St Augustine says that those who say it with confidence will gain the truth, and the false will be annihilated. Say it in the morning before sunrise, 3 times with its Intelligence, 3 days in a row, bending your hand toward the Sun and forming the Character with your two middle fingers.

Name of Intelligence: **CADY**

Its Character:

\\/

PSALM 52.

It is good against the wicked and impious who wish to tarnish the glory of God. If an evil Judge wrongs you, all you have to do is say this Psalm in his presence, if you can, with its Intelligence, and stare him straight in the face with the written Character, and put it where he must go; he will change his intention.

Name of Intelligence: **NEEL**

Its Character:

PSALM 53.

St Jerome says that it is good against hidden and treacherous men. St Augustine says that [he] who says it devoutly will be able to know his friend from his enemy. He who says it will soon confound the slanderers. It serves to hide oneself from the malice of men, by saying it with its Intelligence and folding the big finger of the left hand into the fist, on which one will form the Character as best one can, one will not be caught when enemies want to find the person to do him harm.

Name of Intelligence: **USAM**

Its Character:

PSALM 54.

It is good against the ungrateful, for by its virtue they will be severely punished. It is used to give thanks to God, when we are delivered from peril. It is also good for the Court, like the previous one, by saying it 3 times with its Intelligence and Character, and wearing it on oneself, saying it often. But it is wonderful if you write them both with their Characters.

Name of Intelligence: **NUSY**

Its Character:

PSALM 55.

It makes our enemies fall into the hands of the powers, who will take care of them. Those who say it every day with confidence in God, during their tribulations, will be avenged of their enemies. It is good for weapons, if one writes it with its Intelligence and Character on an iron blade, at the hour and day of Mars; and having written it, one must put it before a fire or the Sun, and afterwards wrap it in coarse cloth and wear it on the collar. Courage will increase and enemies will be terrified, and no weapon will be able to harm you.

Name of Intelligence: **AZAYAIA**

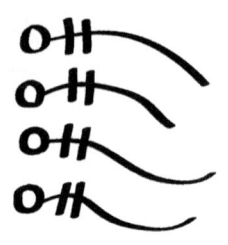

Its Character:

PSALM 56.

It is used to obtain grace and mercy from God, saying it every day. It will make us prosper in our affairs, saying it usually after our ordinary prayers with the Intelligence and Character before us; all things will prosper.

Name of Intelligence: **JOUACH**

Its Character:

PSALM 57.

It is good against Enchanters, Sorcerers and Magicians, who will be severely punished in a short time. It is good against fierce beasts, if said with the name of the Intelligence, making the Character with the 3 fingers of the left hand and showing them.

Name of Intelligence: **NABA**

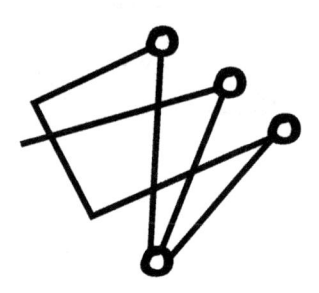

Its Character:

PSALM 58.

It is used to obtain God's help against our enemies, who will be promptly punished. It frees prisoners from a deserved death, saying it with its Intelligence evening and morning, saying: *I pray thee to deliver me, as David made this prayer with its Psalm.* Then write the Character as you may on the wall of your dwelling.

Name of Intelligence: **AZIL**

Its Character:

PSALM 59.

It is good for victory; a King going to war against another Potentate, if it is fair. It is good to deliver a besieged city, if said on a vase full of clear water with its Intelligence, afterwards pour this water in the midst of the city, and trace the Character on the ground.

Name of Intelligence: **KARLI**

Its Character:

PSALM 60.

When David escaped from the persecution of Absalon. It serves to live in prosperity, and comforts us in our adversities. It makes a wife love her husband, if they have had hatred between them, and provided circumstances have been fulfilled and faith is great. It calls back banished people and pilgrims to their country. It is good for an unhappy home, if some ill fate is feared. It should be written on parchment set with Silver, with its Intelligence and Character, and put in an earthen vase and buried in the Courtyard in the middle of the house.

Name of Intelligence: **AOL**

Its Character:

PSALM 61.

It is good for confounding one's enemies, especially those of God, and Princes. It is good for acquiring the glory of God, and despising the world[14], for gaining the necessities of human life, if always said with devotion. It makes one win at gambling if one writes it on Goat parchment on the first Thursday of the Moon, at sunrise, with the blood of a Rooster bled on that same day and hour, and that the parchment is set with Silver. Then write the Intelligence with the Character and wrap it in red taffeta, and carry it with you.

Name of Intelligence: **ITUS**

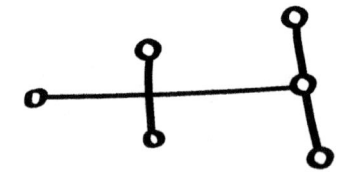

Its Character:

---

14 I guess escaping the world's scorn would make more sense.

PSALM 62.

Whosoever says it devoutly will be filled with blessings for himself and his family, and with spiritual goods. It is used to be loved by a woman. If one says it 7 times, 7 mornings in a row at sunrise with its Intelligence, at a window or door[15], gazing at it fixedly.

Name of Intelligence: **MIZEL**

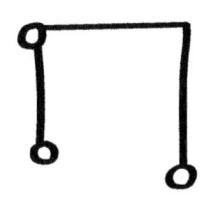

Its Character:

---

15 *À une fenêtre ou porte guarrée,* in the Ms.

PSALM 63.

It is good for getting rid of several enemies, and against the Great who oppress the poor. It converts into faith, into glory, all those who have been in misery, slander and other distresses. It preserves travellers on highways, woods and deserted places from wild beasts, and thieves, and one cannot turn away from his path. To do this, write on the first tree you find the Character and the Intelligence with an iron, then put your hand on the Character and say the Psalm 3 times with the Intelligence; then walk freely.

Name of Intelligence: **PANIM**

Its Character:

PSALM 64.

It is used to obtain God's blessing in order to have abundance of goods on earth, and especially to those who give alms to the poor. If rain is needed, take a vase of ♃ or ☉[16], and form the Character on the sides, then fill it with fountain or river water, then say over it the Psalm with its Intelligence 3 times, and then pour the water over the earth where there are sown plants, saying: *I pray to thee Lord, in accordance with thy power.* And do this 3 times, three days in a row in the morning.

Name of Intelligence: **JYAHS**

Its Character:

---

16 Tin or Gold. Ms. 14784 rather specifies Tin or Silver.

PSALM 65.

David made this Psalm to give thanks to God for having delivered his people from the servitude of Egypt. This is the figure of the resurrection of Jesus Christ and of all the goods of the earth. It should be carried on oneself with the Intelligence, written on Goat parchment, and the Character on waxed cloth.

Name of Intelligence: **MAES**

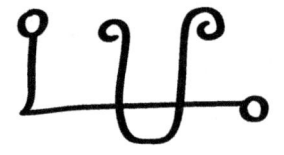

Its Character:

PSALM 66.

Whosoever will say it often with devotion will have goods in abundance, and what is approved in the old and new Law. It has to be said 3 times a day in the new Moon with its Intelligence, and carried on oneself with the written Character.

Name of Intelligence: **GLO**

Its Character:

PSALM 67.

It is good to confound the enemies of the Law, against the dangers of death, and to be delivered from the waters, to obtain the remission of sins and the mercy of God, for the wellness of body and mind, if it is said a few times devoutly. If written on pure white paper, it will put a sick person to sleep if placed on his head.

Name of Intelligence: **JASUR**

Its Character[17]:

---

17   Same Character as Ps. 14.

PSALM 68.

It is good and admirable against lightning and storms, earthquakes, and the inconstancy of the air and sea. It is good against the persecutions of the Church. The poor, widows and orphans who say it devoutly will be delivered, also saying its Intelligence, because the Psalm is the true Orison that Jesus Christ himself said the last 3 years of his life. It is good for travellers, especially at sea, saying it 3 times up to the verse: *Propter inimicos meos redime me.* Then having written it with its Character on a piece of paper and throwing it in the water, one will be delivered[18].

Name of Intelligence: **MAISAT**

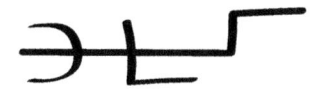

Its Character:

---

18 *Dans un Billet, et Lettre sera délivré*, in the text. However, Ms. 14784 is much more precise and was therefore used here.

PSALM 69.

Whosoever says it devoutly will be delivered from all unforeseen perils. It makes one prosper in all things, if said at the beginning of the canonical hours. It serves to conquer in battle, if worn over the heart, written in blood on the day and hour of ♂ with the Intelligence and Character. And saying it every day, you will conquer all your enemies.

Name of Intelligence: **PALAT**

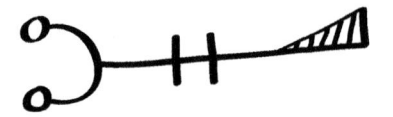

Its Character:

PSALM 70.

It restores vigour to an old man, if written with the Intelligence and Character on a Bear skin. Wrap it in a piece of new cloth, then wear it hanging from the collar in a little Gold box [19], and say it every Sunday and Thursday morning. It will seem that one is getting younger if saying it favourably with great confidence in God, admiring his infinite goodness and clemency, he will be helped and obtain his blessing on him and all his family, and in all their goods.

Name of Intelligence: **JEVEL**

Its Character:

---

19 Ms. 14784 makes it Psalm 69. Moreover, the latter rather indicates: *On a Bear skin or better, on a Snake skin and put next to a Lettuce root. Then wrap it in a piece of new linen and carry it hanging from the collar in a Silver box...*

PSALM 71.

It is good to be loved by all men, and also by Princes and great Lords. It makes us agreeable to everyone. It serves to preserve goods, by writing it on a new piece of earth with its Intelligence and Character. It should be placed under the roof of the house, under a tile so that it cannot get wet.

Name of Intelligence: **ŒHO**

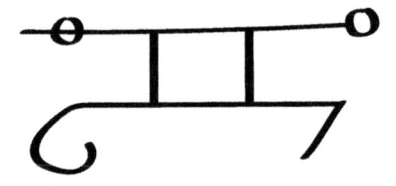

Its Character:

PSALM 72.

It is used to obtain God's grace. It is good for getting answers in dreams. If you say it on Saturday, 3 times while lying down, with its Intelligence and saying your Psalm, make your request and write your Character on an Ivy leaf, and put it under the bedside, and you will obtain a favourable answer.

Name of Intelligence: **ANÉ**

Its Character:

PSALM 73.

It is good for the despaired who believe they have been abandoned by God. It prevents despair if said devoutly at times. It is also good for the Ronz[20] if we say it on the ♃, ♀ & ♄[21] with the Intelligence, having its Character written down and looking at it fixedly while saying this Psalm, and all scandal against Ronz will subside[22].

Name of Intelligence: **DALTI**

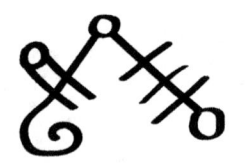

Its Character:

---

20   Thus in the Manuscript. Ms. 14784 clarifies that *Ronz* is intended for: *the defence of Religion,* and further: *all scandal against Religion.*
21   Thursday, Friday, Saturday.
22   See previous note.

PSALM 74.

It serves anyone who says it to be blessed by God. He will be freed from prison like St Peter, St Thomas, and many others who said it every day. It is good for the profit of merchants, if one writes it on the day and hour of Jupiter on a Fox skin with the Intelligence and Character, wrapping it with taffeta bound with Gold thread, and saying it every day.

Name of Intelligence: **RUBA**

Its Character:

PSALM 75.

It is good for destroying the malice of colleges and congregations. St Jerome says he considers it an admirable prayer for obtaining peace and restoring a person who has been stripped of his dignity. It also serves the same purpose as the previous one; and it is good against thunder and earthquakes, if you carry it with you, written in parchment with the Character and Intelligence, and saying it 3 times when it thunders.

Name of Intelligence: **ABIN**

Its Character:

PSALM 76.

It is good for avoiding treachery and destroying those who wish to rise to dignities by evil artifice, and ruin all their intentions. It is good like the previous one, against thunder, [and] insomnia, while lying down saying it 3 times until the verse: *Qui Deus magnificat*, with its Intelligence and putting on one's head its Character well formed on a piece of white linen cloth.

Name of Intelligence: **JARDAEL**[23]

Its Character:

---

23 Or TARDAEL. First letter being much stylized in the Ms.

PSALM 77.

It cures peoples of ingratitude and anger, if devoutly said at the Church, when peoples are afflicted, so that they may be delivered by its virtue. It serves to obtain the friendship of Princes, saying it before seeing them, rising in the morning with its Intelligence, writing the Character in the middle of the left hand. And when you set foot in the palace, look at the Character and name the Intelligence three times.

Name of Intelligence: **CHESDEL**

Its Character:

PSALM 78.

It is proper to pray for the Church of God and its ministers, and for all the faithful, friends and children when it is persecuted. All persecutors are brought down and confounded by its virtue. It serves to be well received by all in our necessities. It is good to be guarded from one's enemies, saying it in the morning with its Intelligence, after the common Orisons, looking at the Character, naming one's enemies, saying: *For thee be it said.*

Name of Intelligence: **CHEMA**

Its Character:

PSALM 79.

If we say it devoutly, when we have planted the Vine, and it begins to produce, it will bear good fruits. If we write it on 4 pieces of paper to the 4 parts of the world, and to the 4 sides of a besieged city, it will soon be delivered.

Name of Intelligence: **ZENAT**

Its Character:

PSALM 80.

It serves to gather good fruits in the coming year, if it is said as taught in the Psalm *Misereatur*. It is used to deliver from slavery, saying it evening and morning with its Intelligence, forming each time the Character by widening the two fingers of the right hand, and bending the tip like a bow, one will be freed.

Name of Intelligence: **JELI**

Its Character:

PSALM 81.

David did this to prevent bad Judges who let themselves be won over by friends, money or hatred. To win one's case, one must say it with its Intelligence before the Court, forming the Character, putting the thumb of the right hand on the left, as you see the Jews say it to preserve themselves.

Name of Intelligence: **SETHA**

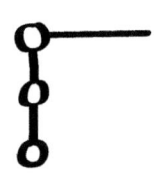

Its Character:

PSALM 82.

It is used against murderers and thieves to stop them. St Jerome says he has seen several experiments. It is also used against those who want to impose taxes on foodstuffs, to earn money at the expense of the poor. This is why, in times of charity, it should be said devoutly every day, to confound usurers and avaricious people. It is also useful for winning in battle, by writing it on a Bear or Snake skin, with the Intelligence and Character, and carrying it with you and engraving it on weapons or the sword; you will see wonders.

Name of Intelligence: **MACAI**

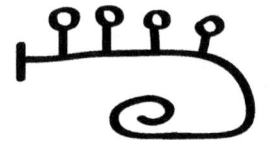

Its Character:

PSALM 83.

Men and women who will say it as they walk through their lands and heritages, it makes them happy; especially on Sundays when prayers have more strength and virtue. It also serves to be received charitably by everyone, and make the fruits of the earth to be preserved, and even our possessions and families. It is also used to say on all occasions and workings, to defeat one's enemies. It calls back the exiles if said 5 mornings in a row with its Intelligence, holding the Character in hand, gazing at it fixedly at the rising of the Sun.

Name of Intelligence: **DEGHAE**

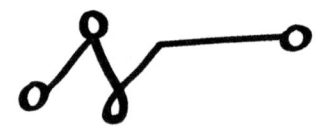

Its Character:

PSALM 84.

The day we say it, we cannot be deceived or oppressed. It brings God's blessing and happiness to all the works of that day. It makes peace between enemies, if we say it in the morning, the Sky being well clear, the face turned to the South, looking at the Sky with its Intelligence and Character, and tracing it on the earth with an iron, then saying: *It pleases you..... to become my friend.*

Name of Intelligence: **HAABIEL**

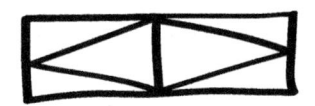

Its Character:

PSALM 85.

David asks God by this Psalm to deliver him from Saul's persecution; that is why St Jerome calls it the venerable prayer, because it is wonderful to deliver us from all our persecutors, if we say it devoutly at this time. It serves against sadness and melancholy, if we write it on Ivy leaves with its Intelligence and Character, and bind it on the forehead as we lie down, saying it 3 times with its Intelligence, and you will be healed.

Name of Intelligence: **MACIEL**

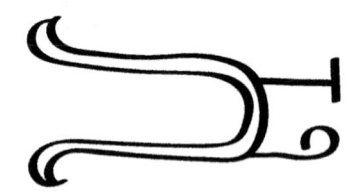

Its Character:

PSALM 86.

It is good to procure the consolation of the neighbour, so that the Church and the ministers may benefit from God's grace. It serves to be loved, if you write it with its Intelligence and Character on the day and hour of ♀ with Pigeon's blood and a Pigeon's feather, on a strip of Goat parchment, attaching it to the right arm and touching with this hand whomever you will, and even his clothes.

Name of Intelligence: **PODUD**[24]

Its Character:

---

24 The Intelligence and Character are the same as Ps. 88. Comparing the two Mss., it is difficult for me to determine which of the two texts is in error.

PSALM 87.

It is used to bring peace with one's enemies and relatives, so that they can agree. It delivers from prison, if written on the door with charcoal or anything black, with its Intelligence and Character. Then touching it with the hand, say it in the morning, at noon, and in the evening, 3 times in succession.

Name of Intelligence: **ASSAC**

Its Character:

PSALM 88.

It makes the States and Kingdoms firm and stable, and also temporal goods, and health of the body and soul, so that whoever says it will have blessing and eternal grace. It delivers friends from prison, if one goes to a clear and uncovered place, looking up the Heaven while saying the Psalm devoutly with the Intelligence, having the Character written before oneself, then saying: *Be....... delivered.*

Name of Intelligence: **PODAD**[25]

Its Character:

---

25 The Manuscript gives the same Name and Character as Ps. 90, namely: ELZADA. The description being identical, I opted for the Name and Character of Ms. 14784.

PSALM 89.

It is good for acquiring wisdom and mechanical science, and for succeeding in all actions. It obtains the blessing of parents and Church leaders in order to prosper. It makes blessings that are to come to someone cannot be prevented. It is good to lift charms and enchantments that prevent a man from living with a woman. It should be written with the Intelligence and Character on a new linen cloth and wrapped in new taffeta; he will heal.

Name of Intelligence: **HACTA**

Its Character:

PSALM 90.

The one who will say it every day will remain in the grace of God, so that he cannot be offended by iron, lightning, pestilence or anything else. The Devil will have no power to harm or tempt him. On the contrary, he will be guarded and defended by the Angels of God. He will not be harmed by any wild, venomous or mad beast, nor by evil Spirits, and will be protected from all things to body and soul, by God's blessing. You have to say it every day and carry it with you. If someone is ill, say it over him, covering him with the Character. If there are Spirits in the house, write it behind the main door; they will leave.

Name of Intelligence: **ELZADA**[26]

Its Character:

---

26 Or ELZADE (Ms. 14784). See note for Ps. 88.

PSALM 91.[27]

It is proper to make one advance to dignities, and temporal greatness as it is said by Joseph, St Augustine and several other Doctors. To do this, it is necessary to take a new earthen vessel, and mark at the bottom the name of the Intelligence and the Character on a Cherry or Olive tree leaf, then fill it with water and say over it the Psalm and name the Intelligence three times, then wash your face with this water and your hands as well, while praying with devotion so that you can obtain what you desire, and recite every morning with your face turned toward the North; you will soon succeed.

Name of Intelligence: **LECHER**

Its Character:

---

[27] Except for a few words, Psalms 91 and 101 are identical. Compared with Ms. 14784, it appears that Psalm 91 is erroneous in the text. The version presented here was therefore considered to be the one authentic.

PSALM 92.

David and Moses also made this one, which is the figure of the Kingdom of Jesus Christ. It increases the faith and charity of men, and maintains peace between those who are in a house. It calms rage and storms on the sea and rivers, if written on a piece of wood with its Intelligence and Character. After reciting it 3 times, throw it into the water.

Name of Intelligence: **JAMIN**

Its Character:

PSALM 93.

It serves against the ungodly who say that God does not lead the world by his Providence. It helps our enemies, it helps the poor, the widows, the orphans. St Augustine says that they will cease to do harm, and that they will be harshly punished, if those in need say it devoutly to destroy unjust enemies. The Intelligence and Character must be written on a piece of bread with a new knife, after purifying oneself with prayers and enemas for 5 days, before beginning the operation on a Monday morning before sunrise, the Sky being clear. You must light some incense and hide in a secluded area, face raised, eyes upward toward the South, holding the Character in your hand. You have to say the Psalm 3 times with the Intelligence, then raise the Character and say 3 times: *God of vengeance, deliver me from my enemies, as thou delivered thy servant David.*

Name of Intelligence: **CANO**

Its Character:

PSALM 94.

St Hierome says it makes us obedient of heart and body. It has the virtue of driving out Demons from bodies, and from all the places they inhabit. It is good for obtaining all kinds of goods and making children obey their fathers and mothers, and draws God's blessing upon them, as well as for converting and driving out the wicked of a city. One must go into the middle of the largest town square and say the Psalm devoutly 3 times with its Intelligence. And [add] each time at the end: *People make amends.* Then trace the Character on the ground with a rod.

Name of Intelligence: **JANNE**

Its Character:

PSALM 95.

St Augustine says that it makes us obtain great graces from God and his Angels, and bring help from the Great and the rich, and we shall have what we desire the day we say it devoutly. If anyone is in deep melancholy, he must write the Character and the Intelligence in the hand with saffron, and put that hand on his heart or head, saying the Psalm and the Intelligence; he will rejoice.

Name of Intelligence: **JAGTI**

Its Character:

PSALM 96.

David composed this Psalm, depicting the judgment of Jesus Christ. It teaches us lessons[28] on how to properly purify our souls, and make the wife live well with the husband, the father with the children, brothers and sisters and friends, and even reconciles them if there was a quarrel between them. It gives advantage in all battles and just wars, enlightens men and all their actions. It serves for joy like the previous one.

Name of Intelligence: **SUMAR**

Its Character:

---

28   *Lections* in the Ms.

PSALM 97.

David made it, like the previous one, to reunite the wife with the husband. It should be written on a large Apple with the Character and Intelligence, name and nickname of the husband and wife. Then cut it down the middle, and afterwards rejoin and bind it with green silk on a ♀ at sunrise, saying: *N.N. companion be joined and may live together very well united.* Put the Apple in their house, in the place where it can best be kept.

Name of Intelligence: **JACAT**

Its Character:

PSALM 98.

It has the same virtue as Psalm 92[29]. It is used to obtain revelation in dreams, if one writes it on parchment, with blue colour, the Intelligence and Character doing it on ♀ and ♄ in the evening before going to bed, and bind it on the forehead, and that one says it without speaking in any way.

Name of Intelligence: **NAZEL**

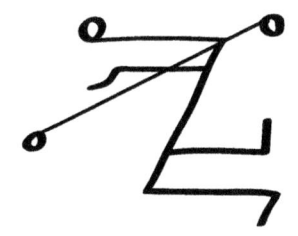

Its Character:

---

29 I cannot find any correspondence with Ps. 92.

PSALM 99.

David made it to be sung by the people with the Angels, at the hour of sacrifice, being seated with our Lord. It serves for the good and the wicked, and to be well received everywhere. On the days when it is said and put behind the door of the Church, where we have prayed unto God, then having put it, we must not stop at the door, and say it with its Intelligence.

Name of Intelligence: **RUTA**

Its Character:

PSALM 100.

St Jerome says this Psalm has the virtue of keeping Kings and Princes fair in their conditions. It turns away spells and evil deeds, especially if said on the day they were done. Moreover, [it] casts out Demons, if said devoutly for three days with the Intelligence, word for word, from the beginning to the end, with the Character in hands. Then no Spirit will be able to stay or offend you.

Name of Intelligence: **ADMIEL**

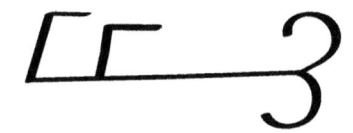

Its Character:

PSALM 101.

St Jerome assures us that he who says it devoutly every day will be wonderfully consoled in all his afflictions. It is used to make a woman conceive. It must be devoutly written on white taffeta and the Intelligence, and the Character written underneath, and all in Dove's blood, and that the woman should always wear it hanging from her collar. And when she lies down with her husband, let her not fail to turn it behind her back between the two shoulders, so that it hangs over the direction of the spine.

Name of Intelligence: **FILTIRA**

Its Character:

PSALM 102.

St Jerome says it gives grace, comforts afflictions, and helps sustain men so that they may glorify God. It makes the husband love his wife, if she writes on parchment at the end of each verse its Intelligence and Character below and above, and wraps it in her hair when she goes to sleep with her husband without his knowing, and he will love her.

Name of Intelligence: **ABA**

Its Character:

PSALM 103.

This one has the same virtue as the previous. St Me Magdeleine said it every day with the previous one, by whose virtue she was consoled with the Angels. St Jerome and St Augustine assure us that those who say it devoutly every day, the Angels will deign to speak with them. It destroys the strength and power of an enemy, if one continues to say it every morning and evening 3 times with its Intelligence, holding its Character before oneself, saying: *I conjure thee, Rontel, that N. have no strength or power over me to offend me, nor to do me any harm, wrong, outrage or damage.*

Name of Intelligence: **RONTEL**

Its Character:

PSALM 104.

St Augustine says that it is admirable; that is why Angels releases prisoners who never stop saying it and praying to God. St Jerome assures us that it has been proven that those who say it with devotion become like the Angels of God, and delivers us from all poverty. It cures Quartan fever if written with its Character and Intelligence on a Deer skin, to be hung on the sick person's collar in the morning, saying it 7 times with its Intelligence.

Name of Intelligence: **COLEAH**

Its Character:

PSALM 105.

This is the second, where there is Alleluia. It is said twice in front of the ₩[30] at the Church, on the day of High Mass, as it is then that Angels and men should sing the praises of God. It is good against Tertian fever, doing as in the preceding one for the Quartan.

Name of Intelligence: **GAREN**

Its Character:

---

30 *Parvis*. Church square.

PSALM 106.

It is good for obtaining the remission of our sins, saying it often with devotion. And according to St Cassiodorus, we will always be free of sickness. [It is] good against continuous fevers, if one writes it with its Character and Intelligence on parchment, binding it to the pulse of the left hand and reciting it three times in the morning, and 3 times in the evening.

Name of Intelligence: **CADAR**

Its Character:

PSALM 107.

It calls servants back to the good graces of their masters, children to their fathers, and wives to their husbands. It is good for obtaining all we want the day we say it devoutly. It makes us prosper in all our affairs, writing it on Goat parchment with Goat blood, on the day and hour of ♃ with its Intelligence and Character, putting it behind the master door.

Name of Intelligence: **ZALCHIS**

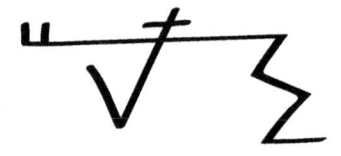

Its Character:

PSALM 108.

It makes God himself avenge us of our enemies. If we say it devoutly, they will be confounded. If you say it out of hatred and malice, you will suffer the vengeance of your iniquities. If we say it devoutly, we will be consoled and will recover the goods that have been stolen; for this is the opinion of all the Doctors who have worked on the explanation of the Psalms, and this after the example of Jesus Christ against Judas and the Jews. If we take a new earthen pot and fill it with fountain or river water, putting mustard in it, then writing its Character on parchment, putting it in the water, saying 3 days in a row 3 times the Psalm with its Intelligence morning and evening over this water, then pouring it over your enemy, taking good care that no drop falls on you.

Name of Intelligence: **JONER**

Its Character:

PSALM 109.

It is used to ask for the grace of Jesus Christ and his Angels, and to pray for the Pastors of one's Church. St Augustine and St Jerome state that to keep one's enemies at peace, one must write it with its Intelligence and Character on plain paper, carrying it on the body and saying it every day at noon.

Name of Intelligence: **SALMON**

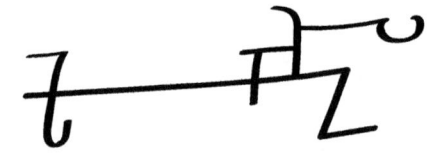

Its Character:

PSALM 110.

It erases our sins and makes us forgiven for our sorrows. It serves to win many friends, if we say it with its Intelligence and Character over Rose water, in the morning, when the rays of the Sun begin to appear and the Character is in the water, engraved on a piece of Apple wood. Then wash the forehead with this water and let it dry by itself.

Name of Intelligence: **ANIEL**

Its Character:

PSALM 111.

It is good to attract blessing for children and on all their actions. They should know it by heart from childhood and say it often. It is proven to give strength and vigour, saying it 3 times a day with its Intelligence, looking toward the East, wearing its Character and Intelligence on parchment sewn into one's belt.

Name of Intelligence: **COAL**

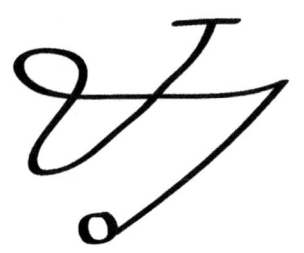

Its Character:

PSALM 112.

It is good not to be offended by infidels, such as Turks and Moors; being for example in Turkey in the main square or near their mosques. You must say the Psalm with its Intelligence, figuring its Character in your mind, and not only will you not be offended, but you will also receive pleasure and honour.

Name of Intelligence: **ELILA**

Its Character:

PSALM 113.

It must be said [devoutly]. It delivers prisoners that were unjustly detained, says St Augustine, that it makes prosper in all things if one writes it with its Intelligence and Character on a blade made of fine ♃ on the day and hour of ♃, and that one puts it on the door, or in the shop. And every morning, say the Psalm with the Intelligence, and your business will flourish.

Name of Intelligence: **REVAL**

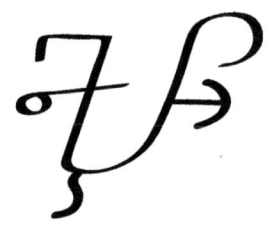

Its Character:

PSALM 114.

It is good for relieving aches and pains from the body, as St Augustine says. It is also good for those who have been wrongly quarrelled, if we write it on new parchment, well prepared and set with Silver, with its Intelligence and Character, wearing it close to the collar, wrapped in waxed cloth, saying it devoutly every morning.

Name of Intelligence: **PILONIA**[31]

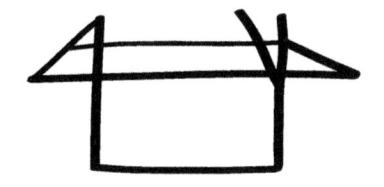

Its Character:

---

31 PITONIA in Ms. 14784.

PSALM 115.

St Jerome says it has such an admirable virtue that whoever says it or has it said for him 3 times a day, until the time he must die, he will be absolved of all his sins. And according to the Hebrews, this Psalm, with the previous one, is one and the same. This is why the Intelligence and Character are the same.

Name of Intelligence: **PILONIA**[32]

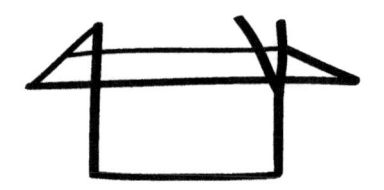

Its Character:

---

[32] PITONIA in Ms. 14784.

PSALM 116.

St Augustine says it is good for destroying the idleness of the lazy, so that they take pleasure in working. It is also useful for an innocent who is persecuted, and for a prisoner. You must write its Character on a parchment, and in the evening at sunset, holding it in your hand while gazing at it, saying the Psalm with its Intelligence. Then saying: *Lord God of truth! Save my innocence; enlighten the mind of him who must judge me so that I may be free and absolved.*

Name of Intelligence: **LUSTEL**

Its Character:

PSALM 117.

It is good against the persecutors of the Church, so that the Pastors who govern it, being held captive, may be miraculously delivered. It is good for the living and the dead.

It serves to be loved in foreign lands, if written with the Intelligence and Character on earth, at the door of a house, village or town, before entering it; and say the Psalm 7 times with its Intelligence.

Name of Intelligence: **ZARTISTA**

Its Character:

PSALM 118.

St Jerome writes that the Blessed Virgin said it every day, because it is the ladder up to the contemplation of God. The 22 letters of the alphabet[33] and degrees in this Psalm. It is also used to obtain the favour of a Judge. It must be written on Goat parchment with the Intelligence and the Character, and when you go to see the Judge, you must look at him fixedly and say the Psalm and the Intelligence.

Name of Intelligence: **CHESTI**

Its Character:

---

33 Hebrew alphabet.

PSALM 119.

It is good for Church and Pastors so that they are delivered and guaranteed from the slander of the ungodly and heretics. If said devoutly, it preserves from the temptations of the Devil, and delivers from the persecutions of the world. St Jerome says that because of its great virtue, it was sung on the second floor of the Temple before the crowd, giving them great consolation. If you find Snakes and other poisonous beasts, you must show the written Character, or picture it in your mind, and say the Psalm with its intelligence.

Name of Intelligence: **NOAS**

Its Character:

PSALM 120.

It is good to go by night in safety, having written it on oneself with the Character and Intelligence, and carrying it always in the hand saying it all the way with the Intelligence.

Name of Intelligence: **PARSI**

Its Character:

PSALM 121.

It is good to be in peace with one's brothers and other relatives; for making the Pastors of the Church live in peace. It is proper for those who wish to speak to Princes, writing it on Goat parchment with the Intelligence and Character. Hold it in your hand, saying it with the Intelligence, being ready to enter the room.

Name of Intelligence: **JORTA**

Its Character:

PSALM 122.

It is used to find something lost, or a valet who has run away. You must write it with its Character and the Intelligence, and say on it your name and that of the lost thing or valet; and also 7 times the Psalm. You'll find them in no time.

Name of Intelligence: **JEUICY**

Its Character:

PSALM 123.

It is used to calm the sea and rivers, having written it with the Intelligence and the Character; carrying it in the hand, saying it for 3 days with the Intelligence and Character before getting on the water.

Name of Intelligence: **MAILAN**

Its Character:

PSALM 124.

It is good for those who travel in foreign, distant and perilous lands, if one puts the Character written in salt, always saying it as one enters and leaves the places to which one is going to and from which one is leaving. Nothing disastrous will ever happen.

Name of Intelligence: **MACOSIA**

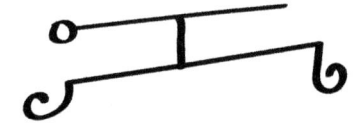

Its Character:

PSALM 125.

It is good to sow the lands of the good people, saying it devoutly; they will reap an abundance of good. It is good for a woman whose children are all dying. It must be written with the Intelligence and Character on 4 pieces of parchment, and as soon as the child is born, one must be placed on the side of the head where he lies, one on the side of the feet, and the other two on both sides, and let the mother say it often. Her children will live.

Name of Intelligence: **JANUI**

Its Character:

PSALM 126.

Those who wish to build any building must write it on a stone with the Character and the Intelligence, and put it first in the foundation and say the Psalm and the Intelligence every day, until the building is completely finished. St Augustine says that all who dwell in it will have an abundance of temporal goods, and will live in the exercise of piety and virtue. He adds that it is admirable for all those who wish to marry, if they say so every day while the proposal is being made to relatives and friends. It preserves children from all harm, if it is written on parchment with the Character and Intelligence, and enclosed in a Silver box, placed on the child, and often said by the father and mother. He will never get hurt.

Name of Intelligence: **JOUCHE**

Its Character:

PSALM 127.

St Jerome says it has the virtue of bringing great spiritual and temporal blessings upon a whole family, if the father of that family writes it on parchment, on the day of ♀ with its Intelligence and Character, and hangs it at the highest point of the house.

Name of Intelligence: **AZLAEL**

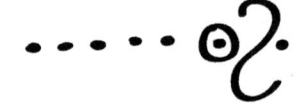

Its Character:

PSALM 128.

It makes us know who are the servants of God, and that we can lose the habit of sin by its virtue. If we fear being harmed, it has to be said 3 days with the Intelligence and the Character traced on the forehead, and we will pass without our enemies seeing us.

Name of Intelligence: **SIMOR**

Its Character:

PSALM 129.

St Augustine calls this Prayer truly penitential[34]. It is useful for the dead on all the Psalms and Graduals[35]. It is good against storms and temptations. And finally, he says that this prayer has always been answered by God, whoever says it devoutly. It is used to obtain revelation in dreams, if one writes it with its intelligence on 3 Cedar leaves, and puts it under the head or bedside table. On entering [the bedroom], let it be said 3 times: *I pray thee Hassard, that this night thou clearly show me the answer to the thing I wish to know.*

Name of Intelligence: **HASSARD**

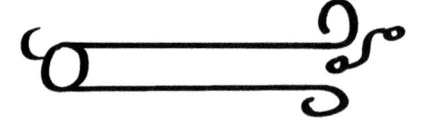

Its Character:

---

[34] *Glenaire* (?) in the text. *Pénitentielle* has been used from Ms. 14784.
[35] The Gradual Psalms, or Ascents, were sung by the Israelites as they climbed the steps of the Temple in Jerusalem (Ps. 119 to 133).

PSALM 130.

We sing it at the 12th degree to ask God for humility, which should be the crown and gem of the ecclesiastics, along with charity. It is good for humbling children, parents, and superb friends, and for making people live chastely, if you say it with devotion and for this purpose. If we feel inclined toward anger and want to correct ourselves, we must write the Psalm with the Intelligence and Character, and write it on plain paper and carry it on the self, saying it 3 times every day, until this passion is entirely extinguished in you.

Name of Intelligence: **SITHY**

Its Character:

PSALM 131.

We sing it at the 13th degree by which God, having seen David's humility, promised him that a son will be born of his wife. And God assures us in this Psalm that he will be the defender of his Church and its Pastors, giving them everything they need. It provides goods, guards and preserves them unto those who say it devoutly. St Augustine says that its great virtue is to make the Church reign and command; that it has more power than the other graduals for the Church. It is also good at keeping and ensuring that an inviolable oath is kept, using it like the previous one.

Name of Intelligence: **CHIUSA**

Its Character:

PSALM 132.

We sing it at the 14th degree. St Jerome says that it gives temporal goods, preserves the friendship of men, which are two things that God figures by the ointment and by the dew, which God exposes in this Psalm; which signifies the grace and abundance of temporal goods that God bestows. Which is why St Jerome urges everyone to always say it immediately with the next; and says that all who say it, not only will always live in the grace and friendship of men, but will also have enough goods and joy; being not able to be punished by shameful or violent death. And it is said that in the early Church, Pope Silvester ordered Christians to say it every day for prosperity in all things. It is good for obtaining peace and keeping it, if one carries it secretly on one's person, written in parchment with its Intelligence and Character, and says it every morning.

Name of Intelligence: **ABRACH**

Its Character:

PSALM 133.

We sing it at the 15th degree, which is the last, and must be joined with the previous one, as it is said, because of the virtues and graces that are the same which will be confirmed by this one with God's blessing. It is also useful for studies, if you write it with the Character on parchment and put it on the book you are studying. And you will retain what you want.

Name of Intelligence: **LIMEDAR**

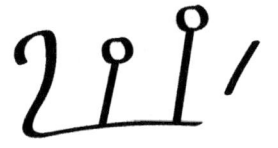

Its Character:

PSALM 134.

If we want our prayers to be answered, we must say them with ardent devotion with the Intelligence, and form the Character with the two fingers of the left hand.

Name of Intelligence: **ECHINIA**

Its Character:

PSALM 135.

It is used to praise the works of the Lord, and to be filled with God's grace. It is good for making long journeys by sea and by land, writing it on blue paper with the Intelligence and the Character, and carrying it on one's person, and saying it evening and morning; one will suffer no pain.

Name of Intelligence: **BILA**

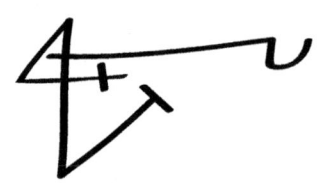

Its Character:

PSALM 136.

If you want to destroy someone's hatred of you, so that they no longer do you harm, write down the Character and the Intelligence and put it in olive oil, and say the Psalm 3 times with the Intelligence on it. Then rub yourself daily with this oil, and speak in front of the hater, and make him stare at you. The hatred will soon be over.

Name of Intelligence: **LAMET**

Its Character:

PSALM 137.

David concludes in the last two verses of this Psalm that sinners will come to penance. St Augustine says it is good for love, if you take some white linseed oil, put the Character in it, engraved on a piece of Cypress wood, and say over it the Psalm with the Intelligence in the name of the person you desire. Then rub your eyebrows with this oil and bind the Character to your right arm after wiping it, and look [the person] in the face, and touch [him/her] with the hand where the Character is attached. You'll be even more successful if you do this on the rising Sun, the first ♀ of the Moon. (It has the same Character as the previous one[36].)

Name of Intelligence: **ANEL**[37]

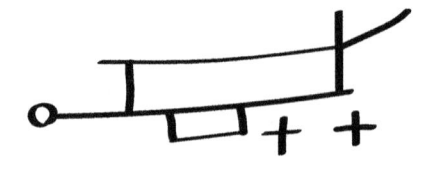

Its Character:

---

36   This phrase belongs to the next Psalm.
37   Should be GRINEL, as corroborated by Ms. 14784.

PSALM 138.

It delivers prisoners who say it 7 times with great devotion. It is used to gain the Prince's good graces, if it is written with the blood of a Goat, on the day and hour of the Sun, with its Intelligence and Character on parchment, and carried on one's person. The Intelligence must be named, having in the morning of the same day, said the Psalm with its Intelligence 3 times.

Name of Intelligence: **GRINEL**[38]

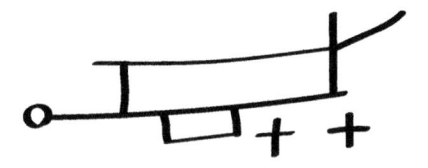

Its Character:

---

38   See previous note.

PSALM 139.

It is good for weapons, if written on a Goat skin with the Intelligence and Character, attaching it to the right arm. You'll be victorious in battle.

Name of Intelligence: **MARNIA**

Its Character:

PSALM 140.

It raises men to the dignities of the world, provided they are true, for truth makes good people reign on earth when they are meek and humble and patient, as St Jerome says. If one falls into deep melancholy, one must write it down with the Intelligence and Character on parchment, and wear it over one's heart saying it every day.

Name of Intelligence: **ALEREL**

Its Character:

PSALM 141.

It will produce the same effects if we say it devoutly through our adversities. St Augustine assures us that it serves against the Spirits of water and earth, and against the afflictions of men and women. Finally, he concludes that he composed it under God's command to instruct us, and to ensure that he who says it devoutly is very much heard in his requests. If someone is imprisoned, he must say it 3 times a day, kneeling with the Intelligence, and forming the Character with the first 3 fingers of both hands, repeating the first verse 3 times, and he will be freed.

Name of Intelligence: **COSFIRA**

Its Character:

PSALM 142.

It brings salvation to the body and soul over all the other Psalms. It is penitential and has great virtues. It is good for travellers by sea and by land, and for those seeking office and dignity. If they are good people, the Holy Spirit will teach them the way they should go, and will guard them on the day it is said. St Jerome assures us that he has experienced this with many others. It is good for those who wish to withdraw from the world or to marry, and to succeed in all things; because the Holy Spirit will lead them by the virtue of this Psalm. It is also [useful] for prisoners, as in the previous Psalm.

Name of Intelligence: **RUSNAM**

Its Character:

PSALM 143.

Those who want to fight justly will be victorious on the day they say it devoutly. St Augustine assures us that he who says it on the day of battle, wearing it on his chest written on a ♄ blade with the Character and Intelligence, will always have the upper hand over his enemies, and will always work wonders.

Name of Intelligence: **AGPAR**

Its Character:

PSALM 144.

It puts the body and mind at rest and brings peace and charity of men. It maintains peace and love between married people, and causes them to give thanks to God for all the blessings. If anyone is worried with any panic fear or terror, any shadow or spectre, write down the Character and Intelligence and put it somewhere on him, without his knowing, and say softly in his ear the Psalm and its Intelligence, evening and morning, for 3 days.

Name of Intelligence: **PACTEL**

Its Character:

PSALM 145.

It can give hope for the same graces that David received with many others who were known on earth and in Heaven. If anyone is wounded, write the Character and Intelligence on parchment, and split it over the wound through the middle, and say the Psalm with the Intelligence over the wound every day, and he will soon be healed.

Name of Intelligence: **MACAS**

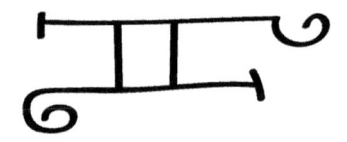

Its Character:

PSALM 146.

It is good to heal the sick who praise God and hope from him to be healthy. If anyone is in extreme need, he should write it with its Intelligence and Character on cotton paper, and carry it with him, and say it every day in the morning, and he will soon be helped by God and men.

Name of Intelligence: **JARCHI**

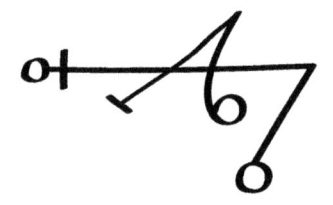

Its Character:

PSALM 147.

St Jerome says it has the virtue of making our temporal and spiritual goods to prosper. And according to the Hebrews, it must be joint with the previous one. This is why it has the same Intelligence and Character.

Name of Intelligence: **JARCHI**

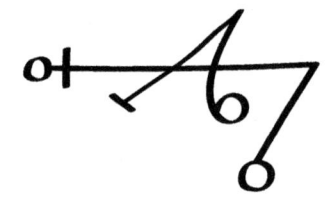

Its Character:

PSALM 148.

Those who will love this Psalm and will say it devoutly will be saved; and those who despise it will be damned. This is why St Jerome says that anyone who wants to be saved must always sing God's praises in this Psalm. It puts out a house on fire, if you write it with its Intelligence and Character on a piece of stone and throw it into the fire saying the Psalm.

Name of Intelligence: **MAIMAL**

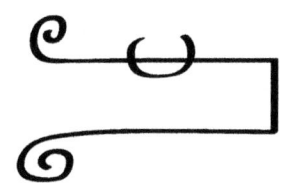

Its Character:

PSALM 149.

St Jerome says it casts out Demons from the body and all other places, and especially from the Church of God, and from a sinful woman. It raises us to honours, if we make ourselves worthy by our prayers and good works, writing it on parchment on the day and hour of the Sun, with the Character and its Intelligence. Carry it with you and say it every morning.

Name of Intelligence: **JACARED**

Its Character:

PSALM 150.

It is good to obtain God's blessing in all things temporal and spiritual. If someone falls into deep sadness, it has to be written on parchment with the Character and Intelligence and carried along on the person, and saying it every morning.

Name of Intelligence: **SINA**

Its Character:

End of the Divine Cabala of the 150 Psalms of David which he composed and left us as a pastoral instruction, for the salvation of our souls and bodies, to worship God and for the assistance we should obtain from temporal goods in the world, according to the examples he has given us, as well as all the good people who followed with all the faithful of the Church of God, who inspired them by his Spirit, so that we may benefit from their virtue for the glory of the Father, the Son, and the Holy Spirit, and for the salvation of our soul, and the good of our neighbour. Amen.

THE 72 NAMES OF GOD
with corresponding verses from the Psalms.[39]

1. Vehuiah
Psalm 3. ver. 4

Tu autem Domine, susceptor meus es, gloria mea, et exaltans caput meum.

2. Jeliel
Psalm 21. ver. 21

Erue a framea, Deus, animam meam, et de manu canis unicam meam.

---

39 Given the variations in spelling in the names of the Genies and to avoid burdening the text with numerous annotations, the reader will consult the *Table of Names of Genies*, at the end of this book.

3. Sitael

Psalm 90. ver. 2

Dicet Domino: Susceptor meus es tu, et refugium meum; Deus meus, sperabo in eum.

4. Elemiah

Psalm 6. ver. 5

Convertere, Domine, et eripe animam meam; salvum me fac propter misericordiam tuam.

5. Mahasiah

Psalm 33. ver. 5

Exquisivi Dominum, et exaudivit me; et ex omnibus tribulationibus meis eripuit me.

6. Jelalel

Psalm 9. ver. 2

Confitebor tibi, Domine, in toto corde meo; narrabo omnia mirabilia tua.

7. Achaiah

Psalm 102. ver. 8

Miserator et misericors Dominus: longanimis, et multum misericors.

8. Cahetel

Psalm 94. ver. 6

Venite, adoremus, et procidamus, et ploremus ante Dominum qui fecit nos.

9. Haziel

Psalm 24. ver. 6

Reminiscere miserationum tuarum, Domine, et misericordiarum tuarum quae a saeculo sunt.

10. Aladiah

Psalm 32. ver. 22

Fiat misericordia tua, Domine, super nos, quemadmodum speravimus in te.

11. Laviah

Psalm 17. ver. 47

Vivit Dominus, et benedictus Deus meus, et exaltetur Deus salutis meae.

12. Haaiah

Psalm 9. ver. 22

Ut quid, Domine, recessisti longe; despicis in opportunitatibus, in tribulatione.

13. Jezaliel

Psalm 97. ver. 4

Jubilate Deo, omnis terra; cantate, et exsultate, et psallite.

14. Mebahel

Psalm 9. ver. 10

Et factus estDominusrefugium pauperi; adjutor in opportunitatibus, in tribulatione.

15. Hariel

Psalm 93. ver. 22

Et factus est mihi Dominus in refugium, et Deus meus in adjutorium spei meae.

16. Hakmiah

Psalm 87. ver. 2

Domine, Deus salutis meae, in die clamavi et nocte coram te.

17. Loviah

Psalm 8. ver. 2

Domine, Dominus noster, quam admirabile est nomen tuum in universa terra.

18. Caliel

Psalm 34. ver. 24

Judica me secundum justitiam tuam, Domine Deus meus, et non supergaudeant mihi.

19. Leuviah

Psalm 39. ver. 2 [40]

Exspectans exspectavi Dominum, et intendit mihi.

20. Paaliah

Psalm 114. ver. [3]-4

Tribulationem et dolorem inveni, et nomen Domini invocavi.

21. Nechael

Psalm 31. ver. 15-16 [41]

Ego autem in te speravi, Domine; dixi: Deus meus es tu; in manibus tuis sortes meae.

22. Iaiaiel

Psalm 120. ver. 5 [42]

Dominus custodit te; Dominus protectio tua super manum dexteram tuam.

---

40 Ms. misstates Ps. 34:1.
41 Psalms and verses missing in the Ms.
42 *Ibid.*

23. MELAHEL

Psalm 120. ver. 8[43]

Dominus custodiat introitum tuum et exitum tuum, ex hoc nunc et usque in saeculum.

24. HAIUIAH

Psalm 146. ver. 11[44]

Beneplacitum est Domino super timentes eum, et in eis qui sperant super misericordia ejus.

25. NITHAIAH

Psalm 9. ver. 9[45]

Confitebor tibi, Domine, in toto corde meo; narrabo omnia mirabilia tua.

26. HAAIAH

Psalm 18. ver. 14

Et ab alienis parce servo tuo. Si mei non fuerint dominati, tunc immaculatus ero, et emundabor a delicto maximo.

---

43 Psalms and verses missing in the Ms.
44 *Ibid.*
45 *Ibid.*

27. Jerathel

Psalm 139. ver. 1 [46]

Eripe me, Domine, ab homine malo; a viro iniquo eripe me.

28. Sæchiah

Psalm 70. ver. 12 [47]

Deus, ne elongeris a me; Deus meus, in auxilium meum respice.

29. Raiaiel

Psalm 53. ver. 6

Ecce enim Deus adjuvat me, et Dominus susceptor est animae meae.

30. Omach

Psalm 70. ver. 5

Quoniam tu es patientia mea, Domine; Domine, spes mea a juventute mea.

31. Lecabel

Psalm 70. ver. 16

Introibo in potentias Domini; Domine, memorabor justitiae tuae solius.

---

46 Psalms and verses missing in the Ms.
47 *Ibid.*

32. Vasariah

Psalm 32. ver. 4

Quia rectum est verbum Domini, et omnia opera ejus in fide.

33. Jehuiah

Psalm 93. ver. 11 [48]

Dominus scit cogitationes hominum, quoniam vanae sunt.

34. Lehabia

Psalm 131. ver. 3 [49]

Si introiero in tabernaculum domus meae; si ascendero in lectum strati mei.

35. Chavakiah

Psalm 114. ver. 6 [50]

Custodiens parvulos Dominus; humiliatus sum, et liberavit me.

---

[48] Missing verse in the Ms.
[49] Ms. specifies Ps. 13.
[50] Verse 1 in the Ms.

36. Manadel
Psalm 25. ver. 8

Domine, dilexi decorem domus tuae, et locum habitationis gloriae tuae.

37. Arriel
Psalm 79. ver. 8 [51]

Deus virtutum, converte nos, et ostende faciem tuam, et salvi erimus.

38. Haamiah
Psalm 90. ver. 9

Quoniam tu es, Domine, spes mea; Altissimum posuisti refugium tuum.

39. Rehael
Psalm 29. ver. 6 [52]

Quoniam ira in indignatione ejus, et vita in voluntate ejus.

40. Jeiazeb
Psalm 87. ver. 15

Ut quid, Domine, repellis orationem meam; avertis faciem tuam a me ?

---

51 Ps. 76 in the Ms.
52 Le Ms. shows verse 1.

41. Hahahel

Psalm 119. ver. 2

Domine, libera animam meam a labiis iniquis et a lingua dolosa.

42. Veualiah [53]

Psalm 87. ver. 14

Et ego ad te, Domine, clamavi, et mane oratio mea praeveniet te.

43. Michael

Psalm 110. ver. 7

Ut det illis haereditatem gentium. Opera manuum ejus veritas et judicium.

44. Jelehiah

Psalm 118. ver. 108

Voluntaria oris mei beneplacita fac, Domine, et judicia tua doce me.

45. Scaliah

Psalm 93. ver. 18

Si dicebam: Motus est pes meus: misericordia tua, Domine, adjuvabat me.

---

53 Genies 42 and 43 are inverted. *Michael* should be 42nd and *Veualiah* 43rd.

46. ARIEL

Psalm 144. ver. 9

Suavis Dominus universis, et miserationes ejus super omnia opera ejus.

47. ASALIAH

Psalm 91. ver. 6

Quam magnificata sunt opera tua, Domine! nimis profundae factae sunt cogitationes tuae.

48. MIHAEL

Psalm 97. ver. 2

Notum fecit Dominus salutare suum; in conspectu gentium revelavit justitiam suam.

49. VEHUEL

Psalm 144. ver. 1

Exaltabo te, Deus meus rex, et benedicam nomini tuo in saeculum, et in saeculum saeculi.

50. DOMEL

Psalm 44. ver. 8 [54]

Dilexisti justitiam, et odisti iniquitatem; propterea unxit te Deus, Deus tuus, oleo laetitiae, prae consortibus tuis.

---

54 Verse 18 in the Ms.

51. Hahasiah

Psalm 103. ver. 31

Sit gloria Domini in saeculum; laetabitur Dominus in operibus suis.

52. Imamiais

Psalm 7. ver. 18

Confitebor Domino secundum justitiam ejus, et psallam nomini Domini altissimi.

53. Nanael

Psalm 118. ver. 75

Cognovi, Domine, quia aequitas judicia tua, et in veritate tua humiliasti me.

54. Nithael

Psalm 102. ver. 19

Dominus in caelo paravit sedem suam, et regnum ipsius omnibus dominabitur.

55. Mehahiah

Psalm 101. ver. 13

Tu autem, Domine, in aeternum permanes, et memoriale tuum in generationem et generationem.

56. Poiel

Psalm 113. ver. 19[55]

Qui timent Dominum speraverunt in Domino; adjutor eorum et protector eorum est.

57. Nemaniah

Psalm 44. ver. 14

Allevat Dominus omnes qui corruunt, et erigit omnes elisos.

58. Jerabel

Psalm 6. ver. 4

Et anima mea turbata est valde; sed tu, Domine, usquequo?

59. Harahel

Psalm 112. ver. 3

A solis ortu usque ad occasum laudabile nomen Domini.

60. Misrael

Psalm 144. ver. 17

Justus Dominus in omnibus viis suis, et sanctus in omnibus operibus suis.

---

[55] Verse 11 in the Ms.

61. Umabel

Psalm 112. ver. 2

Sit nomen Domini benedictum ex hoc nunc et usque in saeculum.

62. Jahhael

Psalm 118. ver. 159[56]

Vide quoniam mandata tua dilexi, Domine: in misericordia tua vivifica me.

63. Anauel

Psalm 99. ver. 2

Jubilate Deo, omnis terra; servite Domino in laetitia. Introite in conspectu ejus in exsultatione.

64. Mehiel

Psalm 32. ver. 18

Ecce oculi Domini super metuentes eum, et in eis qui sperant super misericordia ejus.

65. Damabiah

Psalm 89. ver. 13

Convertere, Domine; usquequo? et deprecabilis esto super servos tuos.

---

56 Verse 59 in the Ms.

66. Mavakel
Psalm 37. ver. 22 [57]

Ne derelinquas me, Domine Deus meus; ne discesseris a me.

67. Eiael
Psalm 36. ver. 4

Delectare in Domino, et dabit tibi petitiones cordis tui.

68. Habuiah
Psalm 106. ver. 1

Confitemini Domino, quoniam bonus, quoniam in saeculum misericordia ejus.

69. Rochel
Psalm 15. ver. 5

Dominus pars haereditatis meae, et calicis mei: tu es qui restitues haereditatem meam mihi.

70. Labamiah
Genèse 1. ver. 6

Dixit quoque Deus: Fiat firmamentum in medio aquarum: et dividat aquas ab aquis.

---

57 Verse 32 in the Ms.

71. Haiaiel

Psalm 108. ver. 30

Confitebor Domino nimis in ore meo, et in medio multorum laudabo eum.

72. Mumiah

Psalm 114. ver. 7

Convertere, anima mea, in requiem tuam, quia Dominus benefecit tibi.

TABLE OF NAMES OF GENIES

Since there are, depending on the sources, certain variations in the way the names of the Genies are written, I thought it would be useful to make this little comparative table to help the reader determine the most appropriate spelling to use for the Genies contained in this little book.

Here are compared the written forms of three sources:
— this present Manuscript;
— the work of Lenain (1823);
— D[r]. Thomas Rudd's Ms. (17th century — Harley Ms. 6483).

	Ms. Fr.14788	Lenain	Rudd
1.	Vehuiah	Vehuiah	Vehuiah
2.	Jeliel	Jéliel	Yeliel
3.	Sitael	Sitaël	Sitael
4.	Elemiah	Elémiah	Elemiah
5.	Mahasiah	Mahasiah	Mahasiah
6.	Jelalel	Lelahel	Lelahel
7.	Achaiah	Achaiah	Achaiah
8.	Cahetel	Cahetel	Kahetel
9.	Haziel	Aziel	Aziel
10.	Aladiah	Aladiah	Aladiah
11.	Laviah	Lauviah	Lauviah
12.	Haaiah	Hahaiah	Hahaiah
13.	Jezaliel	Iezalel	Yezalel
14.	Mebahel	Mebahel	Mebahel
15.	Hariel	Hariel	Hariel
16.	Hakmiah	Hakamiah	Hakamiah
17.	Loviah	Lauviah	Lauviah

	Ms. Fr.14788	Lenain	Rudd
18.	Caliel	Caliel	Kaliel
19.	Leuviah	Leuviah	Leuviah
20.	Paaliah	Pahaliah	Pahaliah
21.	Nechael	Nelébaël	Nelekael
22.	Iaiaiel	Ieiaiel	Yeiael
23.	Melahel	Melahèl	Melahel
24.	Haiuiah	Hahuiah	Chahuiah
25.	Nithaiah	Nith-Haiah	Nithahaiah
26.	Haaiah	Haaiah	Haaiah
27.	Jerathel	Jerathel	Yerathel
28.	Sæchiah	Séeiah	Sheahiah
29.	Raiaiel	Réiiel	Reiyel
30.	Omach	Ornaël	Omael
31.	Lecabel	Lecabel	Lekabel
32.	Vasariah	Vasariah	Vashariah
33.	Jehuiah	Iehuiah	Yechuiah
34.	Lehabia	Lehahiah	Lehachiah

	Ms. Fr.14788	Lenain	Rudd
35.	Chavakiah	Chevakiah	Kevaqiah
36.	Manadel	Manadel	Menadel
37.	Arriel	Aniel	Aniel
38.	Haamiah	Haamiah	Chaamiah
39.	Rehael	Rehael	Rehael
40.	Jeiazeb	Ieiazel	Yeiazel
41.	Hahahel	Hahahel	Hahahel
42.	Veualiah	Mikael	Mikael
43.	Michael	Veuahiah	Vevaliah
44.	Jelehiah	Ielahiah	Yelahiah
45.	Scaliah	Sealiah	Saliah
46.	Ariel	Ariel	Ariel
47.	Asaliah	Asaliah	Aushaliah
48.	Mihael	Michael	Mihael
49.	Vehuel	Vehuel	Vehuel
50.	Domel	Daniel	Daniel
51.	Hahasiah	Hahasiah	Hachashiah

	Ms. Fr.14788	Lenain	Rudd
52.	Imamiais	Imamiah	Aumamiah
53.	Nanael	Nanael	Nanael
54.	Nithael	Nithael	Nithael
55.	Mehahiah	Mebaiah	Mebahiah
56.	Poiel	Poiel	Poiel
57.	Nemaniah	Nemmamiah	Nemmamiah
58.	Jerabel	Ieialel	Yeialel
59.	Harahel	Harahel	Harachel
60.	Misrael	Mizrael	Mitzrael
61.	Umabel	Umabel	Umabel
62.	Jahhael	Iah-hel	Yahehel
63.	Anauel	Anianuel	Anuel
64.	Mehiel	Méhiel	Mechiel
65.	Damabiah	Damabiah	Damabiah
66.	Mavakel	Manakel	Manaqel
67.	Eiael	Elaiel	Eiael
68.	Habuiah	Xabuiah	Chabuiah

	Ms. Fr.14788	Lenain	Rudd
69.	Rochel	Rochel	Rahel
70.	Labamiah	Jabamiah	Yabamiah
71.	Haiaiel	Haiel	Hayiel
72.	Mumiah	Mumiah	Mumiah

TABLE OF INTELLIGENCES

In the light of the variations contained in the two manuscripts used to complete this book, *Ms. Français 14788* for the main text, as well as *Ms. Français 14784* to validate the accuracy of the former, it appears obvious that neither has been copied from each other and that they are the work of two copyists.

As much as possible, I have annotated the major differences in the names of the Intelligences along the way. However, it will be useful for the researcher to be able to consult this Comparative Table of Intelligences at will, in order to quickly find his way around, and to complete his own occult research and experiments.

KEY TO THE 150 PSALMS

	Ms. Fr.14788	Ms. Fr.14784
1.	ELPAD	ELPAD
2.	GHOLAM	CHOLAM
3.	MAGAN	MAGAN
4.	HA	HA
5.	CAMIEL	CANIEL
6.	ISII	ISŸ
7.	EHEB	CLIEL
8.	EJAT	HJIASA
9.	HYASA	EIAT
10.	ZILOZ	ZILO
11.	GABAJH	GABAJA
12.	NEKAH	NEZAH
13.	EATOR	CATOR
14.	ELY	ELY
15.	CAA	CAA
16.	SCEMA	SEEMA
17.	JELA	JELA
18.	MECHEL	MECHEL

	Ms. Fr.14788	Ms. Fr.14784
19.	JEHEU	JEU
20.	MELEE	MELEE
21.	AZLA	AZLA
22.	ASSA	ASSA
23.	COST	COHR
24.	GAMEOL	COHR
25.	JOSLEM	JOFLEM
26.	OMYA	OMIA
27.	JELEM	ZEAM
28.	OLEL	COLEL
29.	DALFA	DALPHA
30.	COSCEL	COSCEL
31.	HELEM	HELEM
32.	JOLA	COLA
33.	RINA	RUIA
34.	EMER	EMET
35.	ALAEL	ALAEL
36.	RAMA	RAMA

	Ms. Fr.14788	Ms. Fr.14784
37.	COLY	COLES
38.	VIQUA	VIQA
39.	PINDAR	LEMDAR
40.	ANENA	AMA
41.	ZACA	ZACA
42.	JEJORDUOSEJOR	SCIOR
43.	ZARIA	SARIA
44.	JEFAVA	JEFACA
45.	ARŸ	———
46.	CAFEAEN/CAFAHEM	CAFEHEM
47.	MALOR/MAZON	MUSOR
48.	SAR	SAR
49.	CAIL	CAIL
50.	JESNU	JESUU
51.	CADY	LADY
52.	NEEL	NEEL
53.	USAM	VSAN
54.	NUSY	NUSILE

	Ms. Fr.14788	Ms. Fr.14784
55.	AZAYAIA	AZAIA
56.	JOUACH	JOUACH
57.	NABA	NABA
58.	AZIL	AZIEL
59.	KARLI	KAILI
60.	AOL	AOL
61.	ITUS	AOL
62.	MIZEL	MISEL
63.	PANIM	PANIM
64.	JYAHS	JAYHIS
65.	MAES	MAS
66.	GLO	GLO
67.	JASUR	JAZUR
68.	MAISAT	MAISAT
69.	PALAT	SEUEL
70.	JEVEL	PALAT
71.	ŒHO	AHOLÉ
72.	ANÉ	ANÉ

	Ms. Fr.14788	Ms. Fr.14784
73.	DALTI	DALTY
74.	RUBA	RABA
75.	ABIN	ABIN
76.	JARDAEL	———
77.	CHESDEL	CHESDEL
78.	CHEMA	CHEMA
79.	ZENAT	ZEUAT
80.	JELI	JESY
81.	SETHA	SETELIA
82.	MACAI	MACHAI
83.	DEGHAE	BAITA
84.	HAABIEL	JANNÉ
85.	MACIEL	DEGATI
86.	PODUD	AABIEL
87.	ASSAC	———
88.	ELZADA	PODAD
89.	HACTA	ASSAC
90.	ELZADA	ELZADE

	Ms. Fr.14788	Ms. Fr.14784
91.	LECHER	LECHER
92.	JAMIN	JAMIN
93.	CANO	CANO
94.	JANNE	———
95.	JAGTI	JAGLI
96.	SUMAR	SIMAR
97.	JACAT	JACAT
98.	NAZEL	NAZEEL
99.	RUTA	———
100.	ADMIEL	ADMIEL
101.	FILTIRA	FILTIR
102.	ABA	ABA
103.	RONTEL	RONTEL
104.	COLEAH	COLEAH
105.	GAREN	GAREN
106.	CADAR	CADAR
107.	ZALCHIS	ZELECHIA
108.	JONER	SONOR

	Ms. Fr.14788	Ms. Fr.14784
109.	SALMON	SALMORY
110.	ANIEL	AUIEL
111.	COAL	COAL
112.	ELILA	———
113.	REVAL	REUAT
114.	PILONIA	PITONIA
115.	PILONIA	PITONIA
116.	LUSTEL	CUSTEL
117.	ZARTISTA	ZARTISTA
118.	CHESTI	CHESTI
119.	NOAS	NOAS
120.	PARSI	PARSI
121.	JORTA	SARTO
122.	JEUICY	SCIUUI
123.	MAILAN	MAILAN
124.	MACOSIA	MACOZIA
125.	JANUI	SANUI
126.	JOUCHE	LOUCHÉ

	Ms. Fr.14788	Ms. Fr.14784
127.	AZLAEL	AZLAEL
128.	SIMOR	SIMOR
129.	HASSARD	HASSAR
130.	SITHY	SILLA
131.	CHIUSA	CHUISA
132.	ABRACH	ABRA
133.	LIMEDAR	LIMEDAR
134.	ECHINIA	THECHINA
135.	BILA	BILA
136.	LAMET	LAMET
137.	ANEL	GRINEL
138.	GRINEL	GRINEL
139.	MARNIA	MARMIA
140.	ALEREL	ALEREL
141.	COSFIRA	COIFIRA
142.	RUSNAM	RUSNAM
143.	AGPAR	AGPAR
144.	PACTEL	PACTEL

	Ms. Fr.14788	Ms. Fr.14784
145.	MACAS	MEAS
146.	JARCHI	JARCHI
147.	JARCHI	JARCHI
148.	MAIMAL	MAIMAT
149.	JACARED	SACAROD
150.	SINA	SINA

APPENDIX.
Pages from Ms. Fr. 14788.

Elohim
Agla
Adonay
Jehova
Schemhammaphoras

Pseaume premier

Par les Pseaumes on peut acquerir la vraie Theologie, l'art de prescher, et de donner bon conseil et prieres pour la conversion des heretiques selon S. Isidore qui le dira 22 jours de suite, et puis après une bonne confession, des bonnes Oeuvres, jeunes, et aumones, verra un Ange de Dieu, qui lui enseignera, comme il doit gouverner ses affaires pour la gloire de Dieu, et son Salut, il sert aussi a eviter les mauvaises compagnies, et trouver les bonnes, il est bon pour la santé, pour estre garanti de la main de ses ennemis il faut l'ecrire sur du parchemin, jusque au Verset ce il y a quiconque = Jeudi a l'heure de Jupiter, puis votre nom, et dessous celui de l'intelligence et son caractere, et ecrive le reste du Pseaume sur du papier de coton bleau turquin, et au dessous le nom de votres ennemis ou contraires, e puis ecrivant = Moi qui suis tes fils de sel ☩

soient

Pseaume 30.

Il est bon contre les Demoniaques, et les puis=
sances Diaboliques, il empeche les malefices,
que les Enchanteurs et Sorciers jettent ordi=
nairement sur les yeux des Enfants pour em-
pecher donc, et detruire le Sortilege il faut
le dire avec le nom de l'Intelligence, sur
de l'huille d'Oliva, et en frotter le front, et
la region du Coeur, et en former le caractere
sur l'une, et sur l'autre il empechera que l'
œil du malade n'ait un malefice, ce qui
arrive assez ordinairement.

Nom de l'Intelligence. Coscel

Son Caractere

Peaume 57.

Il est bon contre les Enchanteurs, Sorciers et Magiciens, qui seront en peu de temps chatiéz severament, il est bon contre les betes farouches; si on le dit avec le nom de l'Intelligence, en faisant le caractere avec le trois doits de la main gauche, et leur montrer —

Nom de L'Intelligence. Naba
Son Caractere.

Pseaume = 82 -

Il sert contre les assassins, et les voleurs a fin de les arrester. S. Jerome dit en avoir vu plusieurs experiences, il sert encore contre ceux qui veulent mettre des imports sur les vivres, pour gagner aux Depenses des pauvres; c'est pourquoi dans le temps de la cherté il faut le dire devotement tous les jours pour confondre les usuriers et avares, il sert aussi pour vaincre dans un Combat l'ecrivant sur une peau d'Ours, ou de Serpent avec l'Intelligence et le Caractere, et le portant sur soi, et le gravant sur des Armes, ou sur l'Epée vous verrez des merveilles.

Nom de l'Intelligence. Macai
Son Caractere.

Pseaume = 94 =

S. Hierosme dit, qu'il nous rend obeissant, et de coeur et de Corps, il a la vertu de chasser les Demons des Corps, et de tous les lieux qu'il habitent, il est bon pour obtenir toutte sorte de bien, et faire que les Enfans obeissent a leurs peres et meres, et attire la benediction de Dieu sur eux, comme aussi pour chasser et convertir les mechants d'une ville ; Il faut aller dans le milieu d'une place la plus grande, et dire 3. fois le Pseaume devotement avec son Intelligence, et a la fin de chaque fois = Peuple aproches toi, puis marquer le caractere sur la Terre avec une Verge —

- Nom de L'Intelligence *Janne.*

Son Caractere ↄZ⊕

Les 72 Noms de Dieu
avec des Versets des Pseaumes qui y repondent.

1. Vehuiah

Pseaume 3. Verset 4.
Tu Domine Susceptor meus es, gloria mea, et exaltans caput meum.

2. Jeliel

Pseaume 21. Verset 21.
Erue a framea Deus animam meam, et de manu unicam meam.

3. Sitael

Pseaume 90. Verset 2.
Dicit Dominus, Susceptor meus es tu et refugium meum; Deus meus sperabo in eum.

TABLE.

Preface to this second edition 5

Introduction 9

Key to the Clavicles of Solomon, of the 150 Psalms of David, with the Characters of all the Genies or Spirits who preside over miraculous operations. 21

The 72 Names of God with corresponding verses from the Psalms 173

Table of Names of Genies 189

Table of Intelligences 195

Appendix 205

Printed in Dunstable, United Kingdom